TEACHING AND LEARNING THROUGH CRITICAL REFLECTIVE PRACTICE

*Anthony Ghaye and
Kay Ghaye*

David Fulton Publishers
London

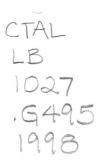
David Fulton Publishers Ltd
The Chiswick Centre, 414 Chiswick High Road, London W4 5TF
www.fultonpublishers.co.uk

First published in Great Britain by David Fulton Publishers 1998
10 9 8 7 6 5 4

Note: The right of Tony Ghaye and Kay Ghaye to be identified as the authors of this work has been asserted by them in accordance with the Copyright, Designs and Patents Act 1988.

British Library Cataloguing in Publication Data
A catalogue record for this book is available from the British Library.

ISBN 1-85346-548-8

Typeset by Kate Williams, Abergavenny.
Printed by The Thanet Press, Margate.

Contents

To our family

Preface

Ask most teachers what the term reflective practice means and they may well reply, 'It's thinking about what you have done'. This book begins with caricatures like this. It then goes on to challenge them and explore other views. It is a book that is intended to help you develop your understanding and skills at reflecting-on-practice. With appropriate kinds of structure, challenge and support it illustrates how individual and collective teaching and learning can move forward with clear intent

The book is based on a model of reflection-on-practice. The model helps you to make sense of teaching and learning. Reflection and action are viewed as a continuous creative and cyclical process. It acknowledges that reflection-on-practice begins with a consideration of different things. It does not let you wander around hoping that you will bump into something that makes sense but focuses attention on professional values, practice, improvement and context. The model then links all of these together.

One of the fundamental purposes of reflecting-on-practice is to improve the quality of teaching and learning. Understanding the role of personal and professional values in this process is important. Values give teachers a sense of professional identity. They also motivate them and provide them with reasons for teaching in the way that they do. The way values are put into practice is therefore explored. Confident, creative and competent teaching is also about reflecting systematically and rigorously on evidence derived from practice. How teachers use evidence to reflect on the quality of teaching and learning is discussed. Reflection is therefore evidence-based.

This is a book about helping teachers improve the way they think and act. This does not occur in a vacuum. It occurs in a changing context. So reflection is not just about self-improvement and self-development but also about understanding and questioning the contexts in which teaching and learning takes place. This can be done collectively and collaboratively.

Tony Ghaye and Kay Ghaye
July 1998

Acknowledgements

Throughout this book we acknowledge the work of many colleagues who have influenced our thinking and practice in many ways. This book is the result of our reflections on their work and on our own practice. In particular we formally acknowledge the support and stimulating dialogues on reflective practice we have had with:

Sam Ansell, Dennis Beach, Phil Chambers, Val Chapman, Jean Clandinin, Brian Clarke, Allan Davies, Derrick Edwards, Hilary Emery, Clive Evans, Margot Ely, Kate Fowler, Jan Francis-Smythe, Ruth Hardie, Graham Hobbs, Chris James, Kevin Jones, Sue Lillyman, Pam Lomax, John Loughran, Geoff Myers, Tess Parkinson, Gail Parsons, Margaret Perkins, Susan Richmond, Helen Roden, Michael Schratz, Jolanda Selvaggi, Stephen Tyreman, Chris Velde, Peter Wakefield, Jack Whitehead, Gill Wilkins, Jianqiang Wu, students on Inital Teacher Training and Continuing Professional Development courses, M.Phil. and Ph.D. programmes at University College Worcester.

Thanks also to Hazel Alley in the Policy into Practice Research Centre at University College Worcester for her help in preparing the manuscript and to John Owens for his encouragement to write and thoughtful comments on drafts of the book.

CHAPTER ONE

The reflective practitioner

> 'I enter my first job knowing what I would *like* to achieve, but also knowing the likelihood of what I *will* achieve.'
>
> (Sam Ansell, Final Year BA (QTS) student)

This was a comment made by a fourth year student when reflecting on her final school experience. Note that she makes a difference between what she wants to achieve and what she thinks she will be able to accomplish. It is a comment from a reflective student who has a confident and developing sense of the kind of teacher she wants to be. Also in her initial teacher training she has learnt that schools can be very different as contexts for teaching and learning. Some of these contexts will be encouraging, stimulating and rewarding while others will be much less so. Becoming a teacher and continuing our professional development is a challenging and complex business. Reflection-on-practice that is structured, challenging and supported is an essential part of this process.

So what does reflection-on-practice mean?

We asked a group of 50 experienced teachers to complete the phrase 'Reflection-on-practice means ...'. Here are some of their responses.

Reflection-on-practice means ...

Navel-gazing	Learning from the day's chaos	Talking about what you do withothers
Learning from experience	Reasoning	Remembering when

Being honest with yourself	Becoming more aware	Constructive criticism
Improving what you've done	Doing it after a lesson	Understanding your feelings
Re-assembling what you do	Questioning yourself	Letting go of personal prejudice
Something done by reflective practitioners	Gaining confidence in your work	Hard work
The latest bandwagon	What you do at college	Dwelling on mistakes
Justifying what you do	Personal growth	Helping you to see what you would or would not do again and why

A conclusion from this is that these teachers thought that reflection-on-practice meant many different things. One comment was that it was something done by reflective practitioners. Another was that it involves reflecting on one's own teaching. There are many views on what reflection is (Bengtsson 1995), what reflective practitioners do and the impact of reflection on the quality of teaching and learning.

For example, some views on what reflection means are as follows. Note some of the things they have in common such as what teachers think, feel and do. Reflection is:

- 'a way of being as a teacher' (Dewey 1933)
- 'intellectual and affective actions in which individuals engage to explore their experiences in order to lead to new understandings and appreciations. It may take place in isolation or in association with others' (Boud *et al.* 1985:19)
- 'a crucial element in the professional growth of teachers' (Calderhead and Gates 1993: 1)
- 'a reaction against the view of teachers as technicians who ... merely carry out what others, removed from the classroom, want them to do' (Zeichner and Liston 1996: 4)
- 'looking back and making sense of your practice, learning from this and using this learning to affect your future action. It is about making sense of your professional life' (Ghaye *et al.* 1996a: 13)
- 'an intentional act of examining the rationale and justification of an action or belief' (Tsang 1998: 23).

This book is intended to help develop your understanding and skill at reflecting-on-practice. Reflection can occur before, during and after a lesson. Reflection on what has been learnt from past lessons can be used to inform current planning. Reflection during the lesson is called 'reflection-in-action' (Schön 1983). This term is often used to describe quite unconscious behaviour and is linked to phrases such as 'thinking on your feet' and being adaptable and responsive to a situation. Eraut (1995b) calls it rapid reflection because it occurs during our interactions with children and colleagues on the spur of the moment. Reflection after a lesson is called 'reflection-on-practice' and is another term used by Schön. It occurs after the event when teachers look back on what has happened. Eraut calls this 'time-out reflection'. The different types of reflection blend into each other, forming continuous cycles of reflection-and-action as teaching progresses.

Many teachers have benefited from learning through reflection and have been called 'reflective practitioners'. Their teaching and their understanding of what is possible and what is less possible, their influence and its boundaries, have arisen from this process. Reflection-on-practice also helps teachers make wise and principled decisions. It is about developing teachers' self-knowledge, the ability to 'see through' teaching situations and understand the meaning of what is happening in their classroom and school. Engaging in the process of reflection is about admitting that practice can always be improved in some way. We can improve the way we nourish the 'good bits' and tackle the 'messy bits'. Reflection-on-practice refuses to let experience become a liability. It takes experience and re-frames the problematic aspects of it so that it becomes workable. Reflection helps establish the improvement agenda for individuals and groups. It can provide teachers with the courage and intellectual capacity to turn insight into improved action. With structure, challenge and support the reflective process enables thinking and practice to move forward. Reflection-on-practice is not just about learning from experience in a private and solitary way; it is about knowledge production that has the potential to enlighten and empower teachers. In this sense it is a creative process. It can help them envision, nourish and imagine improved teaching and learning situations. Reflection-on-practice is done by socially committed individuals and groups. This book is about helping you to appreciate that you do not just have to 'muddle through' on your own.

A few words of caution from the outset. Reflection-on-practice is a complex process. It is much more than 'just thinking about what you do'. Reflection-on-practice is not a toolbox to 'help get you through'. It is a blend of practice-with-principle. It is not always 'safe' but can be threatening as you question your practice. It is about being professionally self-critical without being destructive and overly negative. It is not something to be 'bolted-on'. We are not a reflective practitioner one day a week and some other kind of teacher for the rest of the time. Getting the most from reflecting-on-practice means having a consistently reflective approach to teaching; it is a whole way of being. It cannot just be picked up and put down on a daily basis. A reflective practitioner is a professional practitioner. Reflection-on-practice is not private, self-indulgent 'navel-gazing'. Critical reflection is not a process of self-victimisation but about taking a questioning stance towards what teachers and schools do. It questions the means and ends of education. Reflection-on-practice should not be supported without challenge, for this is hollow. Neither should it be challenge without support, for this can be demoralising. Ideally it needs to be a judicious blend of sensitive support and constructive challenge.

Reflecting on Schön

Schön has made an important contribution to our understanding of reflective practice. In his book *The Reflective Practitioner* (1983) we find a number of key ideas, all of which are woven into this text. They are 'technical rationality', 'knowledge-in-action', 'reflection-in-action' and 'reflection-on-action'.

(a) Schön's work contains a critique of technical rationality, which is linked to the ideas of practice being separated from theory and the teacher being a technician. Schön argues that technical rationality is a dominant way of viewing the relationships between the generation of knowledge and professional practice. Briefly, knowledge is generated in establishments of higher education such as universities and research centres. This knowledge is 'theoretical' and is about how to achieve given ends. Schools are worlds of practice. The teachers' task is seen as applying this theoretical knowledge, from the universities or the 'academy', to solve their teaching problems. It is an application of theory to practice and devalues the knowledge that teachers develop about and through their teaching. Teachers are viewed as technicians because they never question the values that underpin their practice and make them the kind of teachers they are. They never question the context in which they are teaching and how this liberates and constrains what they do.

There are real problems with holding this technical–rational view. For example the ends or products of education are rarely fixed but contested. People have different views about them. Secondly, we have to question the usefulness of knowledge that is produced out of the context to which it is to be applied. Thirdly, the assumption that teaching problems can be solved just by applying someone else's knowledge to one's own practice is simplistic and devalues the art and skilfulness of teaching particular children in particular settings. In this scenario what are teachers to do when they find that, in trying to apply theory to their practice, the theory fails both to solve their teaching problems and explain their practice to them? In the busy worlds of classrooms and schools, 'problems' are many and varied and often difficult to define and resolve. They cannot simply be solved by the application of theoretical knowledge. Schön turns this technical–rational view around and talks about how reflection helps us to pose or 'frame' problems, how we should value and use the kind of knowledge that is embedded in our workplaces, generated by our practice and shared among teachers themselves.

(b) Knowing-in-action is another important idea and is about the professional knowledge that we use in our daily practice. There are two parts to it. The first is that improving teaching and teacher development begins from a reflection on what we actually do, on our own teaching and experience. This reflection generates a rich and detailed knowledge base derived from practice. Our personal and collective teacher knowledge is drawn upon to transform and reconstruct what we do (Valli 1993). The second is that this knowledge is used by us in our teaching. It then becomes knowledge or 'knowing-in-action'. Our knowing is reflected in what we do, how we teach and encourage children to learn. Much of this knowing is often difficult to make verbally explicit (Schön 1987). The knowing is often described as unconscious, tacit and even unarticulated commonsense, but it reveals itself in our teaching actions.

The idea of knowing-in-action is linked to a very different view of theory to that which we described in (a) above. It is a view that, as teachers, we do not just receive and apply someone else's theory to our practice, but we hold and develop our own theories about practice. We have our own personally tailored 'theories' about what does and does not work for us in our teaching. We have theories about appropriate classroom management, effective teaching, meaningful learning and so on. Teachers' work can be viewed in part as 'theory-guided practice'. Carr (1987) sets this out succinctly:

> 'since all practice presupposes a more or less coherent set of assumptions and beliefs, it is, to this extent, always guided by a framework of theory. Thus, on this view, all practice ... is "theory-laden". Practice is not opposed to theory, but is itself governed by an implicit theoretical framework which structures and guides the activities of those engaged in practical pursuits'
>
> (Carr 1987: 165)

Making theory of this kind explicit is important and the chapters that follow should help you do this. Schön develops this idea in his work with Argyris (1992) when they describe their view of a 'theory-of-action'. This again comes in two parts, that of espoused theories and theories-in-use. Our espoused theories are what we say or claim we do, or want to do. We find examples of this kind of theory in lists of lesson objectives and desirable learning outcomes, in school budgets, job descriptions, minutes of school meetings, in school brochures and so on. Theories-in-use, on the other hand, are about what actually happens in practice (note the link here with 'knowing-in-action'). Teachers hold many theories of this kind. Normally we can determine what these theories are by observing teachers at work; their existence manifests itself in the act of teaching. Reflection provides the basis for improvements in our espoused as well as our theories-in-use. The knowledge we have been describing in this section is value-laden and the kind that teachers use to make sense of and to explain their everyday practice.

(c) Reflection-in-action is a third major idea. Schön argued that it is central to the 'art' by which professionals handled and resolved their difficulties and concerns about practice. Reflection-in-action is a reflection on the adequacy of our 'knowing-in-action'. A 'surprise' usually triggers this process, for example, when we begin to realise that our existing stock of knowledge that we are using, our knowing-in-action in other words, is no longer adequate in helping us teach in a competent and confident manner. Reflection-in-action, as the term suggests, occurs in the midst of action. It is based upon a rapid interpretation of the situation, where rapid decisions are required. Reflection-in-action guides further action. Eraut (1995b) looks at this in some detail and in particular at how reflection needs to be further understood in relation to the notions of time-frame (when it occurs) and the context in which it occurs.

(d) Reflection-on-action is the main focus of this book. It consists of reflection after the event, perhaps out of the workplace situation. It is a deliberate, conscious and public activity principally designed to improve future action. Later we argue that this process of the generation of professional knowledge and the improvement of practice, through reflection of one kind or another, can be appropriately described as a research process. The reflective practitioner is a researcher. Reflective practice is a research process in which the fruits of reflection are used to challenge and reconstruct individual and collective teacher action.

An enabling model of reflection-on-practice

This book is about the process of reflection-on-practice, what we might take it to mean, how it might be done, with what intentions and interests in mind. It is also about knowing if reflection has led to any valued outcomes. Two of these are improvements in teaching and learning. Reflection-on-practice is a natural process of making sense of professional action; it is about using and learning from experience. Making sense of teaching is about seeing the process of reflection as a meaning-making process. Not only is this necessary for good teaching, it is also a fundamental human necessity. Baumeister (1991) argues that we find meaning in life by trying to satisfy four needs. These are to do with:

1. *Purpose*   This is about doing things that are satisfying in themselves, such as walking the dog, displaying children's work in your classroom for others to appreciate and listening to children sing in the school assembly. Additionally it is about achieving certain goals and outcomes such as a successful OFSTED inspection or being awarded a professional certificate or degree.
2. *Value*   This is about needs being satisfied by our ability to justify what we do and endow it with some legitimacy.
3. *Efficacy*   This need is satisfied by doing certain things associated with work, personal activities, projects and relationships. This need is also satisfied by the understandings we feel we possess.
4. *Self-worth*   Satisfying this need is linked to our feelings of self-esteem and self-confidence in what we do and believe.

Reflection-on-practice helps us make sense of teaching and learning. Like some other things you will encounter in this book, sense-making sounds obvious and straightforward but is in fact a complex idea and process (Weick 1995). For example, sense-making is a process linked to the way we see ourselves. It is making sense of those things which serve to threaten our identity, reaffirm and repair it. Having to accept early retirement from Headship, changing what and how you teach, or accepting that the promotion you really thought you deserved has gone to someone else, can all threaten our sense of identity. Having a good evaluation of your lesson from a tutor or mentor while on school experience can often reaffirm it. Making sense is also about becoming more aware of the interaction between ourselves and the context in which we teach. Our classroom is a particular context for teaching and learning. We create this environment and we can change it. But context also affects how we act; for example, in small and crowded classrooms only certain non-table or desk-based activities are possible. Making sense is not just a process of having a private conversation with yourself about your teaching, it also involves coming to know through teacher talk and the sharing of experiences. It is an on-going process which requires you to be good at noticing what is going on in your professional world. If events are noticed then we have a chance of making sense of them. For example we need to notice which child keeps talking, which one grips their pencil incorrectly, which ones appear to enjoy reading, who is good at science experiments and talented at playing the recorder.

This book coheres around an enabling model of reflection-on-practice which we have derived from, refined and used in our work with teachers and students (see Figure 1.1).

The model has four characteristics: it is cyclical, flexible, focused and holistic.

1. *Cyclical*   Reflection and action form a continuous cyclical process. By engaging in the process we do not end up back at the beginning! More accurately reflection-on-practice leads us into new and revised cycles.
2. *Flexible*   To be enabling, the model has to be flexible. It does not drag you mechanistically through a series of steps or stages; this is not how it is intended to work. There are two

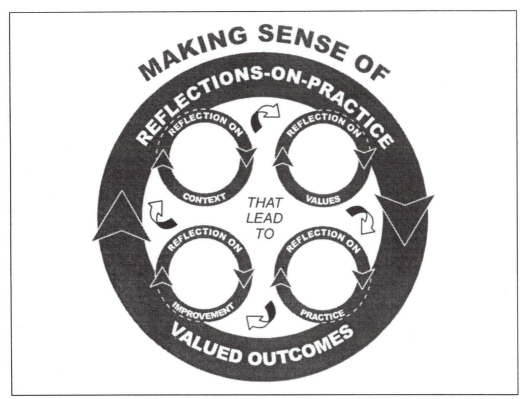

Figure 1.1

reasons for being flexible. First, we begin to reflect-on-practice from different starting positions. For example a teacher might begin with a sense of frustration that she is unable to enhance the quality of children's mathematical experiences in the way she really wants, because of the many and different views on how this might best be done from her colleagues on the staff. Another teacher might reflect on something that she tried out with her children (shared writing) and why it did not appear to work. Another teacher might start with something she believes she wants (more equipment for her children to improve the quality of their science work) but cannot seem to get. Finally, another teacher in a small rural school might want to reflect on the way she develops more effective relationships with neighbouring schools and partnerships with local business and commerce. The different starting points are related to the teacher's values, her practice, on trying to move this forward and improve things, or on the school in the wider community.

The second reason for a flexible model is that it needs to be responsive to the way we learn. Improving teaching and learning does not proceed in a fixed and sequential way; for example, a teacher might choose to reflect on an aspect of her practice first. One thing she might learn is that she gives her children very few opportunities to be more autonomous as learners; she tends to direct, control and manage much of the children's learning for them. Armed with these insights the teacher might then have to reflect on her values and later, if changes in her practice are made, to reflect further on the nature of improvements in her teaching and in children's learning. Another teacher might begin by a reflection on the context in which she teaches; the school might be located in a particularly impoverished socio-economic urban area. Links with parents might be poor, relationships with the community need developing, the school needs to boost its roll, more money needs to be found for staff development and so on. From these reflections-on-context might emerge a consideration of the ways context impacts on practice, which in turn might lead to a reflection on whole-school and teacher values. So values, practice, improvement and context are important to reflect upon. The order in which this is done will vary from individual to individual.

3. *Focused*   Flexibility does not mean wandering around in a morass of teaching problems and concerns hoping to bump into something, at some point, that makes enough sense to get you out of the mess! Focus and direction are needed to enable meaningful learning to take place. Figure 1.1 should be regarded as a map: the 'model-as-a-map' idea means that it helps to direct and focus your attention. It enables you to find your way around, to see ways forward, to understand the educational terrain that needs to be explored. The model has four reflection-action-foci, namely on values, practice, improvement and context. The teacher is free to choose which to focus upon depending on their interests, professional development agenda and concerns.

4. *Holistic*   The model enables you to view teaching and learning holistically. It links professional values with practice, teaching with intentions for improving learning and with professional development. It reminds us that none of this operates in a vacuum but in a changing and often uncertain context.

The chapters in the book relate to each part of the model. After discussing the nature of reflection-on-practice, each of the subsequent chapters explores the four foci in the heart of the model. Within each of the four foci are three key ideas. These are shown in Figure 1.2.

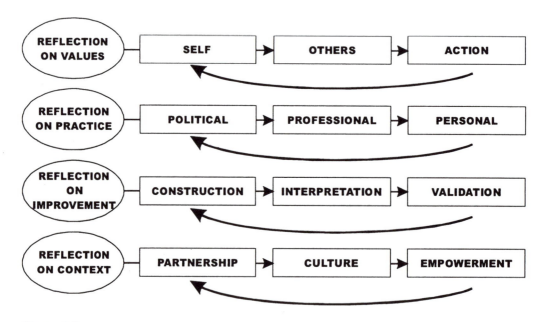

Figure 1.2

Focus: Reflection-on-values

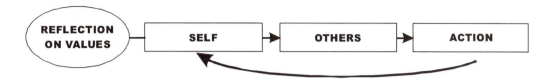

Figure 1.3

It is important to understand the nature and importance of values. Our own values and those of others affect what we do. Values make us the kind of teacher that we are. Our values are things we care about. Teachers try to put their values into practice. For example, if a teacher values pupil discussion because she thinks it helps her children to learn more effectively, she will try to create opportunities for this to happen. Values give us reasons for doing things. We do not all hold the same values; different teachers, schools and Governments can hold very different values. Questions about the choice of particular values and the means to achieve valued outcomes make this whole topic 'contestable'. This focus links the values we might personally hold with those espoused by others. It then makes connections between values and practice.

Focus: Reflection-on-practice

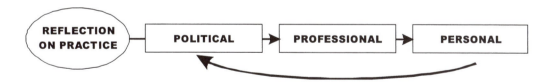

Figure 1.4

Teaching is value-laden practice. Values help teachers to make decisions on how to proceed. But there is also something else. Evidence helps teachers make wise and principled decisions. Confident and competent teaching requires teachers to reflect systematically and rigorously on evidence derived from practice. Reflective teaching and learning then is evidence-based. This particular focus links teaching, evidence and reflection with three things that influence them. These are political, professional and personal influences. Reflection-on-practice is illustrated with reference to the induction of new teachers, the teacher-as-a-researcher movement and the compilation of a personal development profile.

Focus: Reflection-on-improvement

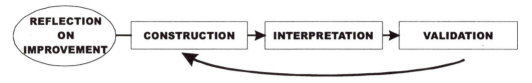

Figure 1.5

One of the fundamental purposes of reflection-on-practice is to improve the quality of teaching and learning. Improvement is a slippery word. It can mean different things to different people. Change is not the same as improvement. Improvements in one aspect of teaching or school life can impair and hold back improvements elsewhere. Improvement is sometimes a trade-off between competing options. This particular focus disentangles improvements in teachers' thinking about their practice from improvements in practice itself. One does not always lead to the other. Understanding something as an improvement is seen to be a meaning-making process. In other words we personally and collectively build or construct our understandings of improvement and this is then linked to the idea of interpretation of reality. Finally, to be more confident that improvement, rather than change, has taken place, the processes of validation are presented. Self and peer-validation are important features of this.

Focus: Reflection-on-context

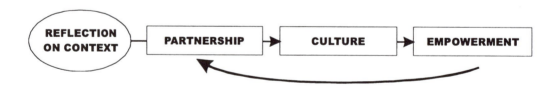

Figure 1.6

Improvements in thinking and practice are one thing; improvements in the context in which these are embedded is something else.Chapter 6 takes a look at the way DfE Circular 14/93 (DfE 1993a) began to change the relationship institutions of higher education have with schools. It is a reflection on the way a Government policy initiative impacts on local practice and in particular the way initial teacher training courses must be planned and delivered in part-nership with schools. Reflection-on-context is a critical look at the way the 'system' serves to influence, constrain or liberate teachers. Critical reflection is relevant here. This is not cynical or negative, but questions the big and complex issues of power, control and the politics of schooling. Values are exposed and questioned and assumptions are challenged. Contradictions between the rhetoric and partnership realities are confronted. Partnership and the school's culture is finally linked to the notion of reflection for more empowered teachers and schools.

One of the central purposes of this book is to empower teachers to take charge of their own meaning-making with the principle 'valued outcomes' being improvements in teaching and learning. For this to happen we have to think about four forms of learning. These are to do with thinking and the way we acquire knowledge and about understanding what we do. This is reflection as thinking about what we are thinking; we can call this *cognitive learning*. Secondly, we have to focus on changes in our feelings and emotions with regard to our work as a consequence of reflecting on it; we can call this *affective learning*. Thirdly, we need to look at what we do as a consequence of what we think and feel; we might call this *action learning or learning from reflection-on-practice*. Lastly, reflection does not have to be a solitary activity. Professional meanings, understandings, insights and avenues for improvement can be acquired through learning from our interaction with others. We can learn by talking to others about our practice, having it challenged, in a constructively critical manner, by our colleagues and by the children we teach; we can call this *social learning*. The enabling model (Figure 1.1) brings all four of these aspects of learning from reflection into an integrated whole. This integration is a creative process that helps move thinking and practice forward. Being creative and being critical is not as crazy as it may sound! The two are not mutually exclusive. In this book being critical is linked with the important process of asking questions about what constitutes appropriate and meaningful teaching and learning. Questioning practice and the context in which it is embedded, if undertaken constructively, supportively and relectively, is a creative process. It is through questioning, that new possibilities for improving the quality of children's educational experiences have a chance to emerge.

CHAPTER TWO

The Nature of Reflection-on-practice

We begin this chapter with a look inside a primary school classroom. Charlotte who is a newly qualified teacher is about to finish her lesson with her class of 30, Year 5 children. It is through reflecting on her practice that Charlotte is able to learn from it. This particular practice incident allows us to begin to establish a vocabulary that teachers might use when trying to talk meaningfully to each other about the nature and purposes of reflective practice. We then extend this vocabulary and build these words into a number of principles, ten in fact, which convey the essence of reflection-on-practice.

Becoming a teacher and continuing our professional development thereafter is a challenging and complex business. We argue that reflecting-on-practice is an essential part of this process. We also argue that at the heart of this process is the reflective conversation. This chapter sets out the characteristics of what might usefully be regarded as a truly reflective conversation, how it might be developed and nourished and some of the things to be mindful of when engaging in conversations of this kind.

The chapter concludes with an excursion into the professional world of Amy, a third-year initial teacher training student, who is reflecting on one of her English lessons with her mixed Year 3/4 class of 32 children. She talks through a lesson with her College tutor. This enables us to make the point that we reflect on practice in different ways. It is not helpful to believe that reflection is simply about looking over your shoulder, going back over things, replaying and rehearsing them in some private, solitary and introspective manner. This is a seriously truncated and skewed view of the nature of reflective practice. The chapter presents another view of reflection, one that is collaborative, public and forward-looking. We illustrate five different and yet complementary types of reflection-on-practice to make this point. Each kind of reflection is a way of making sense of the experiences of teaching and learning.

This chapter therefore does three main things:

- It establishes ten principles that convey the essence of reflective practice.
- It places the reflective conversation at the heart of efforts to improve practice.
- It sets out and illustrates five types of reflection-on-practice.

In doing these things, teaching and learning through reflection-on-practice, whether done individually or collectively, is supportive of efforts to improve the quality of children's educational experiences and the contexts in which these improvement efforts take place.

Look inside and see what's there

It is 10.30 am and time for Charlotte to finish her lesson with her class of thirty Year 5 children. She has been working on the topic of canals. Charlotte recalls:

After this morning's lesson, during playtime, I asked some of the children if they had learned anything from the lesson. Some politely conceded having learned something, others nothing. How can this be! Nothing! The most memorable response came from Billy when I asked, 'Well, what have you learned from the lesson, Billy?' His reply was, 'Eh, something Miss, But I can't remember what it was'.

(Ghaye *et al.* 1993)

Inside this primary school, in the playground in fact, something interesting is happening. Charlotte, who is a newly qualified teacher, is reflecting on her lesson. Billy and the others are 'helping' her to do this. More specifically Charlotte is reflecting on her teaching and on what the children are saying to her about the learning that has gone on. You may think that Charlotte has been pretty courageous to ask her children a direct question of the kind, 'Well, what have you learnt from the lesson?' Alternatively you may want to criticise her timing in asking the question, as the playground is wet and cold and Billy is being strangled by his best friend Tom while trying to eat his way through a packet of Monster Munch crisps! Perhaps you may also think that Billy's response is rather typical, humorous or even an expression of that ageless game some children play called 'guess what's inside the teacher's head'!

If we reflect on this small segment of primary school life further there is much, much more to learn. For in this example there are *people* and there is *action*. Both are located in a *context*, in this case a playground. The people involved have thoughts, feelings, hopes and desires. The action, that is between Charlotte and Billy, is conversational in kind. Taken together what we have here are some of the basic requirements for learning through reflection-on-practice.

Reflecting even more on this, and using different words this time, other things reveal themselves to us. Charlotte is trying to *account for herself.* She is trying to justify her practice by assessing the degree of congruence between her teaching intentions, or now more appropriately called desired learning outcomes, and some pupil feedback. Charlotte is also reflecting on her *experience* and drawing upon the experience of others (her pupils) in order to come to some understanding of the degree to which she might be able to claim that she has taught her lesson on canals in a competent and ethical manner. Charlotte is also showing a certain *disposition* to inquire into her practice. Part of this disposition evidences itself here in a question and answer form. The questions and answers are the beginning of a *dialogue*, or what we might call a reflective conversation, as she starts to tease apart what she has just taught in her lesson before playtime. What is also interesting is that those involved have made *sense* of the lesson, in different ways. Charlotte had a lesson plan; she acted in accordance with it. She communicated her plan and her pupils *decoded* it. In decoding it they were trying to make sense of what Charlotte was saying and of what they were expected to do. After the lesson Charlotte made her own sense of it. She had *constructed* a set of personal meanings about it, some of which seem to sit more comfortably with the pupils' views of it than others!

So there are some big messages here. From a little, if we think about it in particular ways, we can learn a lot. Charlotte's playground behaviour is an example of a *reflective turn*. She is returning to look closely at that taken-for-granted feature of school life, the lesson. Some of her pupils' responses will inevitably challenge her taken-for-granted understandings about her teaching and her assumptions about what her pupils have learnt, or even claimed they have learnt! We can also link this playground action to three other ideas. First, Charlotte must have a reason for reflecting on her practice because normally we reflect on practice to serve a particular purpose; reflection always serves certain interests. Secondly, Charlotte may well be able to improve what she does with her pupils because, through reflection, she has deepened her understanding of what she does, what and how her pupils learn and the appropriateness of the learning context. This deeper and richer understanding may enable her to feel more *empowered to act,* in a particular direction, in the future. Finally Charlotte may feel more enlightened as she weighs up the match between how she teaches, or thinks she teaches and what her children learn, or think they have learnt. Put another way, the reflective conversation in the playground may act as a *bridge* between Charlotte's own *'theories'* about her teaching and how far she puts these theories to use in her *practice*.

From this little example of an aspect of school life some of the key words and vocabulary used throughout this book are to be found. In summary the key words are:

- people (teachers, children and significant others)
- action (that is intentional; there is a purpose to it)
- context (this is where the action takes place and occurs over time. There are other ideas associated with context which we will discuss later)
- accounting for ourselves (this has both a personal and professional dimension)
- experience (what we have done and lived through; we reflect on this experience)
- disposition (as a way of approaching the art of teaching)
- dialogue (the different types of talk that goes on between teachers and their children, children and other children, teachers and teachers and so on)
- sense-making and decoding (this is where we use our powers of analysis, synthesis and evaluation to try to enhance our understanding of learning and teaching)
- construction (the process of building meanings in order to help us to act in competent and ethical ways)
- reflective turns (re-seeing, re-viewing and re-searching what it is we do in order to develop a more holistic view of things)
- empowerment (positive feelings and a developed set of principles that enable us to take wise and appropriate professional action)
- theories (those things which we personally develop or draw upon from the work of others, that help to explain what we do).

What we shall do now is to take this vocabulary, extend it and turn the words into a set of principles. We are going to call these 'principles of reflective practice'.

Principles of reflective practice

This is a book about the practice of teaching and how we might reflect on it, in different ways, in order to improve:

- our thinking about what we do,
- the act of teaching and learning itself,
- the contexts in which teaching and learning take place.

It is a book about and for the improvement of practice. Encapsulated within the phrase 'reflection-on-practice' are a set of principles and processes that, if taken seriously and enacted systematically, have the potential to transform and liberate what we do. The book illuminates around *ten principles* of reflective practice which together provide a view of the teacher as a reflective practitioner. The ten principles weave their way through each chapter and are as follows:

Principle 1

Reflective practice needs to be understood as a discourse (Fairclough 1998). A discourse can be understood as a set of meanings, statements, stories and so on which produce a particular version of events. The reflective discourse, or conversation as we shall call it in this book, is at the heart of the improvement process. Sometimes this conversation has the potential to disturb our professional identity and those things which give our teaching its shape, form and purpose. Additionally, certain types of reflective conversations can disturb the *status quo* by questioning and challenging it. Developing and sustaining reflective conversations in schools is such an important idea that we have devoted a section to it in this opening part of the book.

Principle 2

Reflective practice is fuelled and energised by experience (Boud and Miller 1996, Boud *et al.* 1997, Weil and McGill 1990). We have to reflect on something and that something is our experience and all those things that it comprises. Things such as planning for learning, assessment and recording, class management, teaching styles and strategies and how teaching in the classroom is influenced by what is going on outside or at governors' and parents' meetings, from OFSTED inspection agendas and changes in National Curriculum policy. Reflection-on-practice takes experience and interrogates it in particular ways.

Principle 3

Reflective practice is a process that involves a reflective turn. This means returning to look again at all our taken-for-granted values, professional understandings and practices. This focus on routines, rituals, on everyday occurrences that make up the bulk of a working day is most important. Reflecting on practice is not about reflecting only on the extraordinary, the exceptional and the 'one-off'. In this 'turn' we can reflect on ourselves and the part we played in the particular practice incident. We can also think about the parts played by the significant others involved. In reflecting on ourselves and others we are likely also to deepen our understanding of what it is we are looking at in terms of the practice incident itself. For example we might understand more deeply incidents to do with managing challenging behaviour, differentiating work to suit a range of pupil abilities and appropriate monitoring and recording of pupil progress.

Principle 4

Reflective practice is concerned with learning how to account for ourselves. This means learning how to describe, explain and justify our teaching. This is particularly important in the context of OFSTED inspections where both individual and collective teacher strengths and weaknesses are observed and practice questioned. Similarly, for student teachers, the standards for newly qualified teachers (DfEE 1997) stipulate that all students must be professionally accountable for their practice.

Principle 5

Reflective practice should be understood as a disposition to inquiry. It is not just a collection of methods for eliciting evidence about practice. It is not a toolbox that consists of things such as critical incident analysis proformas, guidelines on how to keep learning journals and conduct school experience debriefs. These are important but should be seen as part of the bigger reflective process. Methods and a sound rationale for their use need to be developed. A rationale can be constructed if evidence-gathering methods are employed to serve more than short-term technical ends. In this book we shall argue that a powerful rationale can be constructed that centres upon the idea of 'reflection as a disposition to enquiry'. The characteristics of this disposition are most often viewed as arriving at the present day via the work of John Dewey and Donald Schön. Having a disposition means that we view teaching and learning 'problematically', that we question it, look into it systematically and continuously strive to learn from it. The overriding goal is to improve the quality of the educational relationships in each classroom, school and other learning environments. Clearly then we do need some kind of toolbox, or set of evidence-gathering methods that work for us in the busy and complex worlds of classrooms and schools, but we should be careful of those who reduce reflection to a set of techniques to be learnt and then applied to practice. We shall argue that reflection-on-practice is about a whole way of seeing and being. It is about having a commitment to the development of a particular professional mindset that enables us to make even wiser and more ethical professional judgements.

Principle 6

Reflective practice is interest-serving, when we reflect we are engaging in a process of knowledge creation. If we are committed to school improvement then, by implication, we are also committed to actually doing something positive and constructive with the knowledge that we create. We need to put the knowledge to work to achieve some desired and justifiable state. So we can argue that we do not just simply reflect on what we do but we do so with certain purposes or interests in mind that need to be served. Different kinds of interest are served by the way we create and use this knowledge. For example, the interests may be personal, professional, political and social ones. It is very important that we sort out in our minds what interests might, or actually will, be served through the reflective process.

Principle 7

Reflective practice is enacted by those who are critical thinkers (Barnett 1997). This can lead to personal and collective improvement through critical forms of reflective practice, which we shall set out fully later in the book. Critical reflection on practice is essentially where teachers acquire a language, a set of arguments, skilfulness and power to transform the existing order of things so as to improve the quality of children's educational experiences. A critical form of reflection-on-practice can enable and empower teachers to act in this way. Central to being critical is the ability to ask probing and challenging questions about what we do. These are often 'why'-type questions. Why do I teach like this? Why did I do it that way? Why has my teaching come to be the way it is? Why do I feel unable to live out my professional values in my everyday teaching? Brookfield emphasises the importance of this principle when he says, 'Being a critical thinker is part of what it means to be a developing person ....Without critical thinking ... our workplaces remain organised as they were twenty years ago' (Brookfield 1995: 1).

Principle 8

Reflective practice is a way of decoding a symbolic landscape. Our everyday taken-for-granted teaching worlds of schools and classrooms are symbolic landscapes. The symbolism is there for us to decode in every aspect of the environment in which teaching and learning takes place. For example in the way classroom furniture is arranged, in what is displayed inside the school, in how people relate to each other, in what is rewarded, recorded and signified as being worthy. These symbols often go together to make up that phenomenon which is often called school culture. This is multi-layered, multi-faceted and a significant influence on the quality of the learning environment. The symbols await professional decoding; reflecting on practice helps us to discern the significance of this symbolism.

Principle 9

Reflective practice sits at the interface between notions of practice and theory. Reflective practitioners have a particular view of these two ideas. Through systematic and rigorous kinds of reflection-on-practice teachers are able to construct meaningful theories-of-action which are in a 'living' form (Whitehead 1993). They are living in the sense that they are made up of reflective conversations and actual teaching episodes, created through retrospective thinking about practice and the public validation of accounts of it. Reflection-on-practice links the account (the 'theory') and the practice (teaching). Linking the two is a creative process.

Principle 10

Reflective practice occupies a position at the confluence or intersection of a number of ways of knowing. Postmodernism is the broad landscape within which this confluence is positioned. A postmodern way of knowing, namely social constructionism, provides some of the bedrock upon which this landscape is shaped. (Burr 1995, Fosnot 1996). This important way of knowing helps the reflective practitioner to construct understandings of the educative potency of their teaching and helps them interpret human action (see Chapter 5).

Summary

Reflective practice can usefully be understood as:

- a discourse
- energised by experience
- involving a reflective turn
- a way of accounting for ourselves
- a disposition to inquiry
- interest-serving
- being carried out by critical thinkers
- a way of decoding the symbolic landscapes of school and classroom
- at the interface between practice and theory
- a postmodernist way of knowing.

The reflective conversation

Becoming a teacher and teaching in a confident, competent, creative and ethical manner is a challenging and complex learning process. Central to this process is our ability to reflect constructively and critically on our teaching intentions, the ends we have in mind and the means we might use to achieve them. The reflective conversation is a medium through which we are able to learn from our teaching experiences and question the educational values that give a shape, form and purpose to what we do. This focus on values is the fundamental characteristic of a reflective conversation. It is one where the teacher interrogates, questions and re-interprets the values that guide what they do, in the context in which they find themselves teaching. Without this quality, we would argue, the conversation is not truly reflective but something else, for example a conversation that is more technically focused. Just as some argue that not all thinking about teaching is reflective if there is no questioning of goals and values (Zeichner and Liston 1996: 1), we would say that it is important to make an early distinction between what does or does not constitute a reflective conversation. Above all else a reflective conversation is one that involves a discussion of values. A focus on values is at the heart of the personal and collective improvement process.

From the extensive literature that exists about the nature and use of conversations and dialogues that serve to introduce and induct us into the 'public discourse of teaching and learning' (Edwards 1996: 143) we propose the following. Each point listed below can be seen as a distinguishing characteristic of a reflective conversation. Taken together we believe they form the basis of what teachers might want to claim as being a truly reflective conversation. These characteristics might evidence themselves, more or less, in each conversation. Some are more easily 'heard' and looked for. Evidence of some is more easily grasped and perhaps recorded. If a reflective conversation is the centre-piece of the whole reflective process, then it seems appropriate to formulate our responses to questions such as, 'So what is a reflective conversation?', 'How far would I recognise a reflective conversation if I heard one?' and 'How might I set about facilitating a conversation of this kind?'

1. To be called a reflective conversation there needs to be some consideration and questioning of the educational values that the teacher is committed to and tries to live out in their work with the children, staff and significant others that comprise the primary school as a community. Our professional values are those fundamentally important things that make us the kind of teacher that we are. They give our teaching its shape, form and purpose. Clarifying, justifying and trying to live these out are things every teacher should strive to do. None of this is easy. Even quite experienced teachers have difficulties in articulating their values and addressing those things that get in the way of putting values into practice. We have given one whole chapter over to these issues in this book.

2. Reflective conversations may initially take the form of private 'conversations with self' but then they should be articulated in public company. In doing this, teachers can try out the language they feel they need so that they can describe, explain and justify practice and when appropriate pursuade, confront and encourage others to question their own practice also. The reflective conversation then is an opportunity for teachers to reflect upon and to shape their own work and in certain circumstances, transform what they do, so as to improve the educational experiences of the children in their care. But this characteristic has additional dimensions worth noting. Moving from the private to the public is often difficult because it implies attaching words to thoughts. Sometimes we stumble around for the most appropriate form of words, particularly if the reflective conversation is about a troublesome aspect of teaching which might involve other colleagues. We might not want to be unprofessional so we pick our words carefully. This private-to-public characteristic is a process of moving from tacit and unconscious knowing (Polanyi 1958) to more conscious knowing. There can be occasions when in trying to facilitate a reflective conversation, we sense that there is, or might be, a hidden agenda which might take quite a bit of teasing out. Sometimes this reveals itself when at the end, or what you think is the end of the conversation, perhaps just as the teacher is about to leave, she turns and says, 'Oh yes, just one more thing.' We often have to be patient and allow time for the real agenda to be expressed. A final point about this characteristic; it can also be used to help us to appreciate what is right and proper to remain private and confidential between two individuals and what should be placed in the public domain because arguably it is in the teacher's best interests and/or in the best interests of the children and the school.

3. The reflective conversation is a special kind of discourse that often takes the form of question and response. The questions can be of many kinds. Some have argued (Smyth 1991, 1995), that there are some fundamental questions teachers should ask if they wish to reveal the nature of the forces that serve to constrain or liberate them. In doing so, teachers give themselves the chance to tackle those things that get in the way of them being able, more fully, to live out their values in their practice. Some of these fundamental questions are:

    *   What is my teaching like?
    *   Why is it like this?
    *   How has it come to be this way?
    *   What are the effects of my teaching on my children?
    *   How can I improve what I do?

The nature of the questions asked is important for they need to enable those engaged in reflecting-on-practice to gain some critical distance on their teaching and the context in which it takes place.

4. In a reflective conversation the participants adopt a 'reflective posture'. This notion comes from the work of Paulo Freire (1972). He described the hallmarks of this posture as conversationalists examining their experience critically, questioning and interpreting it and doing this in a public arena and not in isolation from others. This posture is not one that should be exclusively backward-looking with the conversation being preoccupied with explorations and justifications of previous practice. Reflective conversations should also be forward-looking and be conversations of both possibility and hope. Conversations of this kind contain not only what was thought and done, but what might be or 'that which is not yet' (Ghaye and Wakefield 1993: x).

5. A reflective conversation is located in time and space; it is an artefact of the moment. It needs to be thought about and planned for and time needs to be set aside for it. Additionally the actual timing of a conversation of this kind affects what is, can and might be told. Often reflections soon after the event are very different from those which occur later, perhaps when 'things have cooled down' or simply when the 'teller' has had time to get things into some sort of perspective. Reflective moments need to be created so that conversations of this kind occur (Miller 1990). The 'space' is the socio-political context in which the conversation is constructed. In its public form the space is occupied by at least two persons, the 'teller' and owner of the teaching experience and a significant other. This twosome might be a student teacher and their tutor, student and classroom teacher, school mentor, peer or friend. If one of the goals of a reflective conversation is the development of greater practical wisdom that can be realised in teaching, then the part played by the 'other' is crucial. Pendlebury (1995) calls this person the 'dialogical other' and describes their role as one that elicits the practical arguments and 'theories' that underpin the teacher's work. She goes on to describe the role of the dialogical other as having three parts to it. First, to help the teacher to reflect on aims and means and to develop a particular course of action for her class or individual children. Leading on from this the 'dialogical other' adopts a more critical role and challenges this planned course of action. The teacher then has to erect justifications and address any perceived weaknesses. Finally, and again through conversation, the 'other' facilitates the construction of an improved action plan if indeed one is thought to be necessary and worthwhile. Pendlebury sees the role of the dialogical other in a particular way. It is supportive and one that adds structure to the reflective conversation. But a note of caution. The purpose of a reflective conversation is not solely to focus on weaknesses and deficits; it is not an exercise in remediation. It is important to get things in a balance. Although it is quite natural to want to focus on real and perceived weaknesses, and to know the difference, especially so if you happen to be a student in initial teacher training and on an assessed school experience! It is however just as important to use the reflective conversation to enable the 'teller' to focus upon those aspects of their teaching that are felt to be going well, to articulate the reasons for this and to construct action plans to nourish and sustain the good things.

6. Teachers always have to make sense of their teaching in the situation in which it occurs. They have to make some sense of the perceived and actual impact their actions have on their children and using language is a way of doing this. In reflective conversations an important goal is to try and achieve a greater sense of clarity, rationality and certainty that teaching was done professionally and ethically and what was learnt was worthwhile and

meaningful. It is through reflective conversations that a greater sense of self and professional identity can be brought about. But this sense-making process is one which has to cope with the many possible meanings which can be attributed to any action within schools and classrooms. An important quality of a reflective conversation then is that making sense needs to be viewed as an active and creative process of jointly constructed interpretations (Newman and Holzman 1997). In professional development and particularly in the context of becoming a qualified teacher, reflective conversations, seen as an act of collaborative meaning-making, are an important educational activity. Collaborative knowledge building like this is the driving force for further learning. Through the communication, exploration, challenge and justification of the teacher's 'lived experiences', shifts in perspective, attitude and values may arise. It is through reflective conversations that our established and existing knowledge that guides our teaching can be undone and reorganised to increase its future educational worth. Knowledge generated through reflective conversations is a creative and constructivist process and one 'that construes learning as an interpretative, recursive, building process by active learners interacting with the physical and social world' (Fosnot 1996: 30).

7. The content of a reflective conversation is the teacher's experience. This is what is talked about. We have said that each conversation is located in both time and space; the same can be said of experience. Teaching experiences that are the substance of a reflective conversation do not exist in a social and personal vacuum. Experience is context-related. It is the context which shapes the experience and therefore the learning that is possible. Boud and Miller (1996) have much to say about this.

> Learning occurs within a framework of taken-for-granted assumptions about what is legitimate to do, to say and even think. It is influenced directly and indirectly by the power of others as well as by forces which constrain participants' views of what is possible.
>
> (Boud and Miller 1996: 18)

Learning through reflective practice is centrally about acknowledging the importance of working with experience. In acknowledging this we should be cautious of simply giving primacy to experience without taking into account the context in which, and through which, the experience has come about. Teaching experience should not be celebrated uncritically. In a reflective conversation it is important for the 'significant other' to affirm the student teacher's voice, for example, while simultaneously encouraging the interrogation of such a voice. Teaching experiences can be distorted, self-fulfilling, liberating, suffocating and so on. Simply having experiences to recount does not imply that they are reflected upon in the way we are suggesting in this book. They may be poorly understood and thought about uncritically. The bottom line is that a reflective conversation publically demonstrates a preparedness to be open about the learning that arises from the experience of teaching. It also demonstrates a professional obligation to continue to develop one's practical knowledge. Through conversations of the kind we are suggesting, future teaching possibilities are potentially opened up to us, biases and blind spots can be detected and addressed and the whole 'value-ladenness' of the practice of teaching examined.

8. The final quality of a reflective conversation is linked with the notions of enlightenment and empowerment. We have made the point earlier that it is through conversations of this

kind that teachers' experiences can be interrogated, reconstructed and reorganised. An important objective of the process is to try to add meaning to what the teacher claims to know. This is a vital ingredient for the continual enhancement of professional practice. Some teachers find this process threatening, as their espoused values and values-in-action are questioned, especially if they conclude that improvement is needed. This is why who teachers choose to engage with in this process is an important decision. For students in initial teacher training they may not have such an opportunity to choose. Tutors may be assigned to them for example. Higher education staff involved in school experience supervision and school mentors in our view should be suitably conversant with the principles of, and skilful in, deploying the processes that enable truly reflective conversations to develop. But reflective conversations can also be viewed as empowering.

To help to see this process in this light, the conversation has to be a positive experience. Reflective conversations that are empowering enable the teacher to name, define and construct their own 'realities'; they enable the teacher to sustain themselves. They nourish their sense of professional dignity. They enable teachers to express, in their own way, their authentic concerns. The notions of enlightenment and empowerment through reflective conversations are well put by Elliott (1987) when he argues that teachers should have more opportunities to reflect systematically on, and to confront, their thinking and practices. Elliott argues that the best way to improve practice lies not so much in trying to control people's behaviours, as in helping them control their own by becoming more aware of what they are doing.

The reflective conversation is central to the process of professional improvement and lifelong learning. It counts for nothing and contributes little to enabling teachers to become reflective practitioners if the conversation does not value teachers' own practical theories and lived experiences. It counts for nothing if it does not address the purposes of education in the spirit of openness and constructive critique.

Summary

A reflective conversation has the following characteristics:

- provides a focus on educational values
- moves from the private to the public
- takes a question and answer form
- looks back to what has been
- looks forward to what will be
- is located in time and space
- makes sense of teaching and learning
- interrogates teachers' experiences
- has the potential to enlighten and empower the teacher.

In our discussions with teachers and students a number of things have emerged that are worth setting out here. They fall into the category of 'things to be mindful of when committing oneself to and engaging in reflective conversations'. Some of the most prevalent are thus:

- to give conversations of a reflective kind time to emerge; they need to be worked at, persevered with and nurtured;
- that there needs to be some empathy between the 'teller' and 'facilitator'; each one needs to understand the function of the conversation and the role of the other;
- reflecting-on-practice through conversations is a skilful business which involves feelings, thinking and how these evidence themselves in teaching actions. Some facilitators might need to be trained in this skill;
- it is important that the facilitator does more listening than telling, more guiding, helping and enabling than prescribing and directing;
- there should be some appropriate balance in the conversation between more introspective and contemplative moments and being able to feel that the conversation is going somewhere and that it has a momentum. Time is unlikely to be an infinite resource either for the teller or the facilitator. What counts as an appropriate ending to such a conversation is a crucial issue;
- it is important that both parties understand what the 'ground rules' are for such conversations particularly in relation to ethical, moral, legal and professional issues. Reflective conversations are about people and practice. They can be charged with emotion, judgemental and potentially defamatory. If records of conversations of this kind are kept, then it is important that the nature of the record is agreed between both parties together with where it is stored and who has the right to access it. It is therefore just as well if both parties are clear about issues to do with defamation, litigation, privacy and confidentiality, rights to know, professional mis-conduct and the like. We shall return to these matters later in the book.

Types of reflection-on-practice

Different conversations can give rise to reflections of different kinds. What follows are examples of reflective conversations which illustrate this point. Each kind of reflection is a way of making sense of the experience of teaching and learning. In this book we set out five types of reflection-on-practice. They are based on our work with students and teachers and called:

- descriptive reflection-on-practice
- perceptive reflection-on-practice
- receptive reflection-on-practice
- interactive reflection-on-practice
- critical reflection-on-practice.

Each kind represents a dominant way in which a teacher might reflect upon their work. For example 'descriptive reflection-on-practice' means that teachers are able to offer descriptions of what they do. 'Receptive' kinds of reflection-on-practice includes being open or receptive to other and alternative views which can help teachers to justify what they say and so on. These five types do not represent a hierarchy but ways of expressing and making sense of practice.

The main issues at stake here are as follows. The first is that reflective conversations have to be developed. Their quality varies and this can be as a result of many things such as how used the participants are to learning through conversations of this kind and how much experience of teaching the 'teller' has. Not surprisingly then reflective conversations can exhibit different characteristics. Not all are penetrative, constructively critical, forward-looking, felt to be empowering and the like; it takes a while for them to mature into this form. Some conversations may be rooted, anchored and even locked into elaborate descriptions of 'what is', or perceived to be, rather than anything else. The conversations which follow show some of these different qualities. They have been linked to the five different kinds of reflection-on-practice set out above. We have also said that it is a focus on values that is a fundamental characteristic of a reflective conversation. In each of the conversations that follow there is a values dimension. Sometimes it is more clearly and explicitly discernable than in other conversations. Although we discuss values in the next chapter it might be worth stating here that knowing, then articulating and justifying our professional values is a challenging business. In the following conversations two things should become apparent: that teaching is a value-laden activity and that some teachers are more conscious of their values and of trying to live them out in their daily work than others.

Three further points of clarification. First, different conversations held over a period of time can show evidence of the same or different kinds of reflection-on-practice. Secondly, within the same conversation, say between a student teacher and her tutor, there may be evidence of one dominant kind or evidence of different kinds of reflection. Part of the tutor's skill is to detect these different kinds of reflection and then to enable the student to appreciate the dominance of one or more when talking about their experiences. An additional role for the tutor is try to get the student to draw upon other kinds of reflection depending upon the context and the purpose of the conversation as it unfurls. Thirdly, it is unwise to see these types of reflection as being mutually exclusive and as tight, almost watertight, compartments. A reflective conversation is a fluid and dynamic phenomenon. It is important to appreciate that as it develops, reflections-on-practice might naturally evidence more or less of one kind of reflection or another. The purpose of delineating each type is to allow the teller and facilitator to appreciate more richly what is being reflected upon, in what ways and how further insights and learning might accrue if teaching is reflected upon in other ways. So another central message that is emerging in this book is that reflection-on-practice is much, much more than that encapsulated by the often-stated cliché, 'Reflection is just simply thinking about what you do!'

A lesson with Amy

Amy is a third-year student on an honours degree course in Primary Education. She is working in a mixed Year 3/4 class of 32 children. She has been with the class for two weeks. This is her first full week of teaching the whole class and she is looking forward to the challenge.

She has planned and carefully thought through an English lesson. Her desirable learning outcomes are clearly stated in her plans and she is confident that the lesson will go smoothly. Her National Curriculum focus is 'writing', with a particular emphasis on writing for a specific audience. She is also hoping to address speaking and listening skills. During the lesson Amy will be observed by her tutor. She will then have the opportunity to discuss her teaching afterwards. The intention is for the tutor and student to engage in a reflective conversation.

The particular activity which Amy has planned involves the children working in groups of four, writing a collaborative story for a child in a Key Stage 1 class. The children have already met their 'audience' and have discussed the types of story that each child enjoys reading. Amy has looked at a variety of books with her class and discussed page layout, illustrations and vocabulary. She feels very satisfied with her preliminary work and is confident that her children are now ready to begin to write their story.

She introduces the lesson to the whole class and then divides them into groups of mixed ability, each group including children from both Year 3 and 4. Amy gives each group a large piece of paper and a pen and encourages them to 'brainstorm' and write their ideas on the paper. After 20 minutes she feels they should be thinking about beginning to write the story. Each group has to get one child to act as a scribe. By the end of the lesson Amy hopes that each group will have agreed both the content and structure of the story.

Once Amy has explained the purpose of the lesson and how she wants the children to work, she tries not to intervene in each group's work. She monitors the noise level, positions herself at the teacher's desk and decides to take the opportunity to hear individual children read. She calls them to her, one by one, glancing up from time to time to monitor the group work. She deduces from this that the children are busy, that discussions are taking place, that most of the children appear to be 'on-task' and that there seems to be a positive working atmosphere in the classroom. Amy is therefore pleased that her tutor is observing a well organised, cooperative group work activity.

After 20 minutes, Amy reminds the children that they should now be choosing a member of the group to act as scribe. They have a further 40 minutes to put their collective ideas into a story form. She continues to hear children read and responds when the children ask for help. From time to time she moves around the classroom and pauses to check that each group is busy. The noise level is occasionally rather high and so Amy asks them to work more quietly. Throughout the lesson her tutor takes the opportunity to speak to some of the children and observe each group. Amy's School Experience file is read and her tutor writes comments in it.

Five minutes before the end of the lesson Amy asks the children to stop working and to tidy up. They are told that they will be able to continue with their stories the next day. The class responds sensibly and waits for the dinner bell to ring. At lunchtime Amy has the opportunity to discuss the lesson with her tutor and to look through the children's work.

A reflective conversation with Amy

What follows are extracts of the conversation that Amy had with her tutor. It was tape-recorded so that Amy could reflect on it further if she so wished. The extracts that have been selected illustrate one particular kind of reflection which we call descriptive reflection-on-practice. The hallmarks of reflections of this kind are that it is a personal, comprehensive and retrospective account of teaching. It is essentially a description of a lesson, or part of it. Few justifications are offered for the way in which Amy teaches. It serves to place teaching in a context and therefore contains reference to what was taught, where, when and with whom. Conversations that are predominantly descriptive reflections-on-practice may also have a sense of history about them as the 'teller' refers to past events. These may be what she has done before with her present class or with other classes. This kind of reflection is the teller's view of what happened. In this case it is Amy's version of events.

In order to help Amy to learn from her experience, her tutor asks her a series of questions. The purpose of these questions is to gently 'deconstruct' Amy's teaching. This deconstruction involves pulling it apart, sensitively and patiently, in order to explore it. Deconstruction does not mean destroy. On the contrary, the tutor's intention is to try to enable Amy to become more aware of what she is doing and why her teaching is the way it is. As we have said, this can be a time-consuming process and may not be fully or satisfactorily achieved in the context of an immediate post-lesson conversation and just before the tutor rushes off to the next school and other students. Reflective conversations require much skilfulness on the part of the tutor and a preparedness, by Amy, to engage in such a conversation, openly and positively with her tutor. We are now beginning to touch upon some of the 'big ideas' of John Dewey (1933) when he argued that reflective teaching requires attitudes of open-mindedness, responsibility and whole-heartedness. We will pick these up again later.

We have selected five of the questions that Amy's tutor asked. We believe each one can be taken as an invitation to Amy to reflect on what she has taught. You should try to match up Amy's responses to what we are calling *descriptive reflection-on-practice* and in doing so bear in mind the caveats mentioned earlier.

Tutor: 'Amy, I noticed that you structured your lesson to involve the children working in mixed-ability groups. Why did you decide to do this?'

Amy: 'I thought it would make a change for the children to work in groups with Year 3 and 4 together. I tried this on my last teaching practice and it seemed to work well. So it seemed commonsense to give it a go again on this practice. They don't have many opportunities to work on a group task and so I decided that I would plan an activity which would help them to work together.'

Tutor: 'Your plans show clearly what your learning outcomes would look like. How far do you feel you have achieved them?'

Amy: 'I think the class knew what was expected of them and I can see that they have all produced something. They've put their ideas on paper and they seem to have made an attempt to start the story. They seemed to be getting on with it in the right sort of way.'

Tutor: 'How do you see your role in today's lesson?'

Amy: 'I wanted the children to work on their own as much as possible. I don't think they need the teacher interfering all the time because it can put them off. So I decided to listen to readers because I've seen the class teacher take opportunities to do this whenever she can. I've seen how she does it.'

Tutor: 'How successful do you think you were at monitoring the children's learning?'

Amy: 'Well, I kept an eye on the class and I made sure they were all busy. There was a bit too much noise at times and so I tried to quieten them down. I think it worked. They all looked interested in the activity and there was lots of discussion, especially between Emma and Nicky who don't normally get on well.'

Tutor: 'What have you learned from the lesson?'

Amy: 'I think the children can work together in groups but maybe I could organise the classroom better. I think four in a group is fine. I'd do this again I think. I was pretty happy with it.'

Created conversations

Earlier we said that conversations can show evidence of different kinds of reflection-on-practice. In addition to 'descriptive' there are four other types of reflection. They are:

- perceptive reflection-on-practice
- receptive reflection-on-practice
- interactive reflection-on-practice
- critical reflection-on-practice.

In order to illustrate the qualities of each, we have 'created' four further conversations that Amy might have had with her tutor that day. We have taken the same five tutor questions, that refer to the same lesson, so that you can compare the conversations more easily. These created conversations act as evidence to show the different (and additional) ways Amy might have reflected on her lesson.

Perceptive reflection-on-practice

When reading this second conversation through, a number of different qualities emerge.

Tutor: 'Amy, I noticed that you structured your lesson to involve the children working in mixed-ability groups. Why did you decide to do this?'

Amy: 'I feel very strongly that these children need to work in groups from time to time. Each child has a different strength and I feel that the rest of the group should appreciate that. I like children to learn from each other so I tried to give them the opportunity. It pleased me to see children cooperating at this age and I wanted to give them a chance.'

Tutor: 'Your plans show clearly what your learning outcomes would look like. How far do you feel you have achieved them?'

Amy: 'Well, I feel very satisfied with the outcomes. It's a shame that they can't carry on this afternoon. I was pleased that they cooperated. I felt I coped OK with the readers and at keeping one eye on the rest of the class. I wondered if the "brainstorming" bit might get out of hand but I needn't have worried because they came up with some good ideas.'

Tutor: 'How do you see your role in today's lesson?'

Amy: 'I must admit to being very comfortable in my role. More comfortable than I thought I might actually. I really wanted the children to be able to get on independently, to talk amongst themselves and decide how they would write the story. I really didn't want to intervene in case I inhibited them. I feel quite strongly about this. I like listening to the children read, helping and encouraging them. I was a little worried that it could have gone wrong because they do depend on me, too much I feel.'

Tutor: 'How successful do you think you were at monitoring the children's learning?'

Amy: 'Well, I did feel pleased with the way the lesson progressed. It went according to plan. No real hiccups I thought that made me panic. The noise did concern me a bit though. I think they enjoyed the lesson and when that happens, I enjoy it too.'

Tutor   'What have you learned from the lesson?'

Amy: 'That the children are keen to try out new ideas and like to work in different groups. That they can have fun when they are in school and still be learning something at the same time. That I can organise a lesson like this and actually enjoy it too! Yes, it was a good experience I thought.'

What counts as evidence of *perceptive reflection-on-practice* is when the 'teller' makes a demonstrable link between descriptions of their teaching and their personal feelings about it. As a teacher it is only natural to have both positive and relatively more negative feelings about yourself, other colleagues and about the school in which teaching and learning take place. Reflective conversations of this kind convey such things as passion, joy, aggression, puzzlement, sadness and appreciation. The conversation links together teacher thinking and feelings. Just like descriptive reflection-on-practice this kind also involves the process of deconstruction and is about thinking back and going over things.

Receptive reflection-on-practice

The first two types of reflection-on-practice are retrospective, personal accounts, essentially descriptive in nature and associated with feelings about how well teaching was felt to have gone. They are egocentric in the sense that they are Amy's own view of things. In this third type of reflection-on-practice further qualities evidence themselves.

Tutor: 'Amy, I noticed that you structured your lesson to involve the children working in mixed-ability groups. Why did you decide to do this?'

Amy: 'This is something that I've wanted to try for a long time. I've read about the different ways of grouping children and I've seen some really good lessons by other teachers who believe in mixed-ability group work. I thought I was ready to give it a go, especially after talking with the class teacher about the mix of abilities in each group. I'm not sure that I got the mix right for every group though. It's not quite as straightforward as some books make it out to be!'

Tutor: 'Your plans show clearly what your learning outcomes would look like. How far do you feel you have achieved them?'

Amy: 'I need to spend some more time looking at what the children have produced but I know that at least one group did achieve the targets and they have now written a good story outline. It's got a clear beginning, middle and end. That's one success but I'm wondering if they would have achieved more for someone else, like their own teacher. I'll ask her later. Some of the children said they enjoyed the lesson but I must admit I was disappointed by others' efforts. There are definitely things I need to work on.'

Tutor: 'How do you see your role in today's lesson?'

Amy: 'To be honest I was in a bit of a dilemma with this one. I wasn't sure whether to mingle with the children throughout the lesson or whether to follow my teacher's example and listen to some children read. Bearing in mind the time that it takes to do this, I'm not sure which is a more effective use of my time. Too much control by me and the children don't think for themselves and get dependent. Too little control and some of them start floundering while a few others just exploit it and try to mess around.'

Tutor: How successful do you think you were at monitoring the children's learning?

Amy: Well, I have seen this lesson taught in a similar way by a teacher in my previous school. She seemed to have it down to a fine art, all the children worked really well and she knew what each group was doing. I'm not sure that I did actually monitor them carefully enough. Perhaps they are not as independent as I thought they would be at this age. Or maybe it's just different for them and they need to adjust to my way of teaching.

Tutor: 'What have you learned from the lesson?'

Amy: 'The most important thing is that this activity is a lot more difficult to put into practice than I imagined. It seemed a simple idea but planning took ages. And you have to expect some of the children to disagree with each other or want to write their own stories without using everyone else's ideas. It's OK in theory but ...! Also they said that they haven't had much experience of this way of working, you know in teacher-less and more cooperative-type group work. The class teacher doesn't do much of it. She told me so. They need practice at it. I think I'm much more aware of what I need to do now.'

What counts as evidence of *receptive reflection-on-practice* is when the 'teller' clearly relates their view of the world and their construction of classroom reality to that of others. They are receptive and open to alternative perspectives. What makes this a different kind of reflection from the two previous kinds, is that the teller offers, through the process of the reflective conversation, clear justifications for practice derived and synthesised from her own and other people's views of things. The teller reflects in such a way that they bring forward evidence in order to authenticate and justify their practice. So this kind of reflection has some important qualities. It is reflection that generates practical knowledge that is 'positioned'. By this we mean it is knowledge that is positioned or aligned in relation to some wider and more complex picture. This picture would include the experience of other teachers, the professional literature in the form of journals, books and magazines and practitioner research. In receptive reflection-on-practice the teller critiques what they claim to know. The emphasis is on reconstructing practice in such a way that new possibilities for action arise out of new insights.

Interactive reflection-on-practice

This type of reflection-on-practice has a quality about it that is not present in the other three conversations.

Tutor: 'Amy, I noticed that you structured your lesson to involve the children in mixed-ability groups. Why did you decide to do this?'

Amy: 'Well, I thought the children needed an opportunity to work in a different learning situation and with children who they do not normally choose to work with. I thought this would be a good learning experience for them. I've only been with the class for two weeks so I am still getting to know them. I don't think each group was as carefully balanced as it might have been. Next time I think I need to make sure that each group has at least one competent writer in it, someone who enjoys drawing and a balance, where possible, of boys and girls. I don't know the children's characters well enough yet, but I think I know what changes to make next time.'

Tutor: 'Your plans show clearly what your learning outcomes would look like. How far do you feel you have achieved them?'

Amy: 'This is difficult to assess at the moment. I know that some groups took far too long on the first part. I'm not sure that I can just expect them to "brainstorm" unguided, in 20 minutes and get all the ideas down on paper. I think I might structure that a bit more next time. Also the big paper and felt-tip pens were a novelty to many, it seemed. Maybe we could have more of a whole-class discussion first or maybe in the groups, individuals or pairs, could write their ideas down on separate pieces of paper. Then they could all be placed in the middle of the table, read out and then they could try to agree on the best four or five. I'm semi-pleased with the outcomes but I also think I'll have to sort out how I can help the group with Jamie in it to start to write the beginning of their story. They can't decide.'

Tutor: 'How do you see your role in today's lesson?'

Amy: 'I deliberately planned to give particular children some quality reading time while the others were working. I did not intend to keep them away from their groups for too long in case they felt they missed too much. It didn't work as well as I'd hoped. Some were reluctant to leave the group to come out to read. Others stayed longer than I had planned. When Sophie and Ben went back to their group they were greeted with a bit of hostility. They couldn't get back into it. Sometimes I also had a queue at the desk from those asking for help. Then I thought I should get up and move around. Next time I'm going to try to manage the middle part of my lesson better. If I have to juggle different roles then I don't want to get stressed out or lose control of the class.'

Tutor: 'How successful do you think you were at monitoring the children's learning?'

Amy: 'They knew that although I was listening to readers, I was also keeping an eye on them. In future I think I would stop the class, from time to time, and ask for one person to update me on the progress of each group. That way I would know if they were keeping on-task. The noise level did get up a bit. Well, it was too noisy at times. I've got to stop the "nagging" bit. You know, always saying "come on work more quietly please". I'm aware of this and I think I need to make my expectations clearer. I might give some of the children a chance to catch up at playtime if they want to. I'm going to work some of this into my next lesson and see if things improve.'

Tutor: 'What have you learned from the lesson?'

Amy: 'I've definitely learned that, despite how carefully you plan and how well you prepare, things can still go wrong or not run as smoothly as you would like. I need to be more realistic and appreciate that every day will have its ups and downs. I think I also need to be prepared to adapt my plans. This is a big thing with me, having a clear plan and yet being able to be flexible. I'm going to talk to my class teacher about this. She knows the children and I need to build some of this experience into my planning.'

What counts as evidence of *interactive reflection-on-practice* is when the 'teller' articulates the links between learning from their teaching experience and future action. This kind of reflection is not only a process of looking backwards but more significantly a process that is forward-looking. It takes the learning that has arisen from other kinds of reflection and begins to put it to work. Interactive reflection-on-practice organises past learning, future intentions and teaching rationales in the form of an articulated action plan. These plans show how imagined solutions to improve teaching are justified in terms of moving individual or collective practice forward. This kind of reflection also makes clear the part others might play in enhancing future practice. The past is not irrelevant. What has been learnt is paramount. What is to be done with this learning is centrally what interactive reflection-on-practice is about.

Critical reflection-on-practice

In this last type of reflection-on-practice a questioning tone should be clearly evident.

Tutor: 'Amy, I noticed that you structured your lesson to involve the children working in mixed-ability groups. Why did you decide to do this?'

Amy: 'This is a teaching strategy that I've used successfully with children before. I've noticed that the practice in this school does not usually encourage mixed-ability grouping. But the class teacher was willing to let me try, so I'll have to keep her in touch with how it's going. I believe that children should have the opportunity to work together, to collaborate and share their skills with other children because as they get older they will have to work with different people and get on with them.'

Tutor: 'Your plans show clearly what your learning outcomes would look like. How far do you feel you have achieved them?'

Amy: 'Well all that stuff about leadership, giving children clear roles and responsibilities and independence to be creative is important. Some might say, "Well, I don't think the children have done much today!" Some groups haven't got a lot written down but I would argue that they have in fact been really busy, thinking and discussing. I'd argue that learning doesn't necessarily have to find its way into the children's folders at the end of each lesson. I believe that process is as important as product. But I do feel that the school puts me under pressure to produce something for parents. I feel I've achieved something perhaps that I didn't expect. That all learning outcomes are not visible and concrete and if you go for that all the time, you have to compromise on other things.'

Tutor: 'How do you see your role in today's lesson?'

Amy: 'It was a combination of teacher direction, at the beginning, with independent work in groups. I'm aware that listening to children read while the others are working might be criticised by some teachers. I'm in a bit of a difficult situation. The school expects every child to be listened to, on an individual basis, once a week and I knew that I was running behind schedule. The school's reading policy is clear on this. Also my reading records have to be completed by Friday. This is a pressure so I decided to fit in some more readers. I'm sure there is a better way to manage this expectation especially now that we have the literacy hour. I'm not happy with how I help children to read and the system just adds to the pressure. Reading is given priority in this school. I'm not sure that I agree with it. I'm not sure I did the right thing. I want to be fair to all the children.'

Tutor: 'How successful do you think you were at monitoring the children's learning?'

Amy: 'I think I could have monitored things more closely. But I bet everyone says this. I don't know. Well, your question makes me think, about my management, the noise level, leaving them to get on and the rest. Am I contradicting myself? It seems that I want everything, doesn't it? I believe independent working is good for the children but with direction. That I want a quiet classroom but I can't insist on one, don't want to and especially if I want the children to work independently. I believe that the children should be given lots of opportunities to discuss things, talk through things in their own way, and yet I'm also anxious that they have something down, you know, something to show for it.'

Tutor: 'What have you learned from the lesson?'

Amy: 'I think I was over-ambitious and that I needed to support and encourage all the children more. I think I should have taken opportunities to get the children to share their work with the rest of the class as they progressed because I really believe that children should learn from each other, should listen and ask each other sensible questions. These are lifelong skills after all, aren't they? Trying to get them working effectively in groups, in this school and on teaching practice is all a bit ambitious, I think. But I'm still going to try. The children aren't used to group work. I know what I believe in but actually putting it into practice on TP is more than about you. If the school or class teacher is not supportive, then you have to be prepared to say one thing and not be able to put it into practice. You've got to get the teacher and the children on your side. If the teacher is a bit awkward or sees what you do as threatening, then you've got to explain why you want to try something out. Sometimes this takes a lot of guts. Sometimes you have to be prepared to make compromises. With my group work I'm trying to emphasise children's self-discipline and collaboration. But the teacher thinks there's no discipline because they're all doing their own things and because I'm not in the role of authority figure.'

What counts as evidence of *critical reflection-on-practice* is when the 'teller' begins to question accepted routines, classroom practices and school rituals. Here 'why-type' questions are being asked and answered. They are asked with reference to the teaching of individuals and groups of teachers. In doing so the *status quo* is being challenged. Criticism should not be confused with cynicism, destruction and negativity; critical reflection has the intention of being creative and constructive. The values that guide teaching are exposed but questioned and not taken for granted. Assumptions made about effective teaching and effective schools are opened up to debate and critique. Contradictions between what is perceived to be educational rhetoric and teaching realities are confronted. This can be quite threatening for some.

Critical reflection-on-practice cannot be meaningfully undertaken without an understanding of and a willingness to confront the big and complex issues of power and politics in schools. It is a kind of reflection that is about the individual teacher, the individual as part of the whole-school culture, and how their teaching might be transformed in order to improve the quality of the educational relationships she has with her children. But it is understanding how the quality of individual action is influenced, constrained or liberated by 'local' structures and the 'system' within which the teacher works. The system is made up of many parts and includes policy from the Department for Education and Employment, the Teacher Training Agency, the Qualifications and Curriculum Authority, the influence of Local Education Authorities, teacher unions, governing bodies, parents and so on. Teachers are not 'free agents' to do just as they please. Teachers work within local, regional, national and international systems which serve to guide and influence what they do and provide opportunities for growth and development. These systems which are, for example, political, cultural, economic and professional in kind, can also serve to constrain, devalue, marginalise and disempower teachers. Finally, critical reflection-on-practice is also dependent upon other kinds of reflection we have already described.

Summary

Reflections-on-practice can be of different types. Five types are:

- descriptive reflection-on-practice which is personal and retrospective
- perceptive reflection-on-practice which links teaching to feelings
- receptive reflection-on-practice which relates your view of things to others' views
- interactive reflection-on-practice which links learning with future action
- critical reflection-on-action which places individual teaching within a broader 'system'.

CHAPTER THREE

Reflection-on-values:
Being a Professional

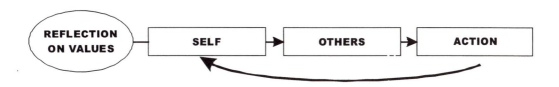

What kind of teacher am I?

This is a challenging question. You should not be drawn into thinking that this is a simple, obvious and straightforward one to answer. To answer it we have to be honest with ourselves and have an ability to reflect on what we do and why we teach in a particular way. Describing what we do is a good starting point; after this we need to move on to trying to explain and then justify our teaching, both to ourselves and to others when called upon to do so. Our values play a key role in this process.

Throughout our teaching careers we think, behave and believe in certain things, such as how far our teaching can be called 'educational', about what we can offer children and what our capabilities are. What we do, think and feel about teaching constitute our sense of professional identity. We can reveal and communicate this identity when we address and articulate an answer to the question, 'So what kind of teacher am I?' To begin to tackle this question we need to look at what we do. Sometimes teachers talk in specific terms. For example, 'I am a specialist in teaching English and I am very confident in assessing and diagnosing children's reading skills through the use of miscue analysis with my Year 2 class.' At other times teachers may convey what they do in more general terms. For example, 'I try to give every child in my Year 2 class the opportunity to achieve their full potential.'

Describing what we do is a good starting point in exploring the issue of being a professional. In doing this we are often making the tacit explicit (Day 1991, Polanyi 1962). This is a process where we make the things that give our teaching its shape, direction and purpose more conscious, more knowable and therefore more open to inspection and critique. If we reflect on these descriptions of practice, we give ourselves the chance to learn from our experiences of teaching. This can help to move our practice forward.

If we look at our own teaching or if others observe what we do, we should expect to see an effort being made to put into practice what we value. We might not always achieve this to our full satisfaction; knowing our values is therefore very important. But this process of knowing is not always an easy one. Often this knowing remains rather unconscious. We often hear teachers say 'we do what we do but we are not that good at articulating why we do it that way'. Our professional values therefore provide us with reasons for teaching in particular ways.

At University College Worcester we ask all final year primary school students to undertake an assignment where they have to respond to the question 'What kind of teacher do I want to be?' In this account they have to state and justify their professional values. We subjected the scripts of 140 students in 1997 to content analysis and found that many values were being expressed and in many forms. These values were to do with things such as being enthusiastic and stimulating, being tolerant, fair and respectful, praising and encouraging children and so on. Five common value 'clusters' emerged which arguably gave this cohort its sense of purpose and professional identity:

1. *Developing a sense of community*, for example, consideration for other people, trust, honesty, cooperative learning, belonging and togetherness.
2. *Exercising care and compassion*, for example, with regard to enhancing pupils' self-esteem, being fair, genuine and making pupils feel secure through clear rules and routines.
3. *Fostering pupil self-determination and participation*, for example, through developing autonomous learning, self-reliance and a sense of pupil empowerment.
4. *Respect for human diversity*, for example, pupils being valued as individuals, treated as equals, curriculum differentiation, pupil identity and rights, interpersonal acceptance.
5. *Professional demeanour*, for example, being committed, passionate, reflective, enthusiastic, motivating, approachable, trustworthy and a good listener.

Interestingly, some of these values are scrutinised as part of OFSTED inspections and the way schools help to develop pupils' 'attitudes, behaviour and personal development'. For example, inspectors look out for the extent to which pupils:

- behave well in and around school, are courteous and trustworthy and show respect for property,
- form constructive relationships with one another, with teachers and other adults and work collaboratively when required,
- show respect for other people's feelings, values and beliefs ... show initiative ... willing to take responsibility (OFSTED 1995a: 17).

In clarifying your allegiance to your professional values you might find that you are in a state of 'dynamic equilibrium'. By this we mean that you do not become attached to one set of unchanging values but that your values tend to move around and become modified as you develop more experience and insight and as the contexts in which you work change. As we search for greater self-undertstanding, more robust rationales for what we do and greater consistency in trying to live our values out in our teaching, a sense that all our values are static and fixed entities may be far from our lived reality. Our values can and do change. This is quite natural. We believe that at the point of career entry, student teachers need to have a set of personally-owned professional values, that they can articulate and defend, and know how to respond in school when encountering others who hold conflicting and alternative values equally as strongly as themselves.

> We cannot base our work together for the common good on reticence, embarrassment and incoherent mumbling, yet this is the state into which the discussion of morals and values has descended in many parts of Western society today. The main culprit is the popular cultural assumption that to try to define something as good and right in an absolute sense is an unwarranted and potentially oppressive incursion into a domain which should be purely private. What is right is simply what feels right to me. What is good is simply a matter of individual opinion.
>
> (Carey 1997: 3)

In order to be called professional and to be convincing about what we do, we have to reflect on what we are doing and be appropriately responsive to what is happening around us in our classroom and school. However, it is no good for teachers to simply say that they are doing a good job: proclaiming this is not enough. Good practice needs to be demonstrated. The art of teaching is one that needs constant renewal and reworking. In order that it does not disintegrate, it is imperative that this process coheres around a set of educational values that can be justified by being held under constant review and communicated clearly and convincingly. A teacher's values should be derived from the nature of what constitutes effective and ethical practice. To reach this position we have to understand and question the purposes of education.

> The assumed relationship between values and practice stands in need, then, of considerable qualification and refinement ... The values implicit in ... practice have to be actively sought out and acknowledged. From this perspective, teaching is a profession only insofar as the educational values it espouses in theory are professed in – and through – its practice. The prime task for teachers as professionals, therefore, is to work out their educational values, not in isolation and abstraction but in collaboration with colleagues and amid the complexities of school life.
>
> (Nixon 1995: 220)

Teresa is an experienced teacher who has created a description (Lehane 1992) of some of her work with her children who have profound and multiple learning difficulties. She expresses her values in the following way:

Value 1: 'I believe children's experience of school should be happy and positive. To profoundly handicapped children the education system and the classroom can be fairly meaningless ideas.'

Value 2: 'I want children to achieve. Before 1970 they were considered "ineducable" and excluded from the education system ... I am committed to the children's progress and education as opposed to care alone.'

Value 3: 'I also believe in the child-centred interactive approach where children are encouraged to follow their own interests and wishes through play and interaction and where education aims to enhance experience and personal growth rather than simply building up skills or knowledge.'

Teresa's values illustrate why she works with children in the way she does. Our professional values therefore provide us with reasons for teaching in particular ways. The following scenario in Teresa's classroom describes her practice and her reflections on the way she relates to one particular child.

Kevin is nine years old. Teresa introduces her account with a brief sketch of him, a sketch which she radically redraws after reflecting on her teaching and asking herself a modified Smyth (1991) question. She does not think it appropriate to ask the initial question suggested by Smyth namely, 'What do I do?' but, in the context of her teaching she argues that the question, 'What do *we* do?' is more appropriate and powerful. This is Teresa's early thumb-nail sketch of Kevin.

> *Kevin is 9 years old and cortically blind but walks with help and splashes around the swimming pool with armbands. Kevin can communicate and although his speech is limited and repetitive he makes relationships with his carers. Kevin needs and demands a great deal of attention. He explores the environment with his hands but is unaware of his own strength, cheerfully destroying playthings. Kevin needs help to feed himself with a spoon. He is doubly incontinent and epileptic.*

In one account of part of her work with Kevin called 'one wet Tuesday afternoon', Teresa describes how she is trying to teach Kevin to locate and move towards the sound of an audible ball. Teresa placed a video camera on a tripod in the corner of her classroom. She often video-taped some of her teaching so that she could reflect upon it later, interrogate it and get a better sense of herself as a teacher. Teresa later reflected on her teaching and called the account that she wrote from watching the videotape, 'Missing the best bits'. Here is an extract from that account.

Missing the best bits

Work with Kevin starts abruptly with me announcing, 'We'll go and find your ball.' ... When he then moves from crouching to a high kneeling position I say, 'good kneeling', but on reflection Kevin's action looked like a communicative gesture of joining in than mere motor action. Later when the toy organ stops working and I say so, Kevin says 'oh dear' ... again I missed it perhaps because Kevin often says this as a catchphrase. However on this occasion the words were meaningful and deserved a response to underline the fact.

I omit to let Kevin feel the ball at the start of the activity, one of his few ways of working out what is going on. Kevin successfully locates the ball. I reward him with an enthusiastic, 'good boy, well done' but did not reinforce the meaning of the situation by saying what he had done. The task is only one of seeking, not of doing anything with the ball.

I missed opportunities to engage Kevin's attention and activity. When guiding him to the ball I could have asked him to give me his hand rather than just grasping it. I do not control background noise for a task in which audibility is crucial and I leave Tim (and James) without input for minutes at a time. When moving away for a few moments to 'troubleshoot' I do not explain this to Kevin and leave and return unannounced, potentially unnerving for a blind child.

There is a beautiful snatch of film where Kevin and James interact with each other, a notoriously rare event for children with profound and multiple learning difficulties. To my shame, although I am working with Tim, I clearly see this happening and yet I take no affirming action and intervene simply to take control when the contact becomes rough. This effectively ends the interaction.

The contact begins with Kevin trying to further inflate a silver balloon (the inside of a wine box). Kevin rustles it. James snatches at and rustles it and then Kevin rustles it again and pulls it away. James shrieks and then Kevin pats him on the back, pulling the smaller child towards him. I could intervene sensitively at a number of points, for example I could encourage James to echo the pat on the back. Instead I simply pull the two boys slightly apart with the words, 'stop fighting'. On continued replaying of the video it can be seen that after initially pulling James, Kevin says, 'be careful', as if telling himself and then becomes gentler an instant before I intervene.

(Lehane 1992: 55–56)

There is much to learn from this account. It is only through a commitment to reflect on her teaching that Teresa is able to become more aware that she is, in her words, 'missing the best bits'! Her account shows us how Teresa is putting some of the principles, described in Chapter 2, into practice. For example through reflection she is becoming aware that she could look at her practice in different ways (Principle 1). She knows that what she does with her children will serve certain interests such as educational and personal ones (Principle 6). She is looking at videotapes of her own teaching which enable her to ask questions about what she is doing, or thinks she is doing (Principle 7)! Teresa is also convinced that by doing these things she might see her teaching in new and different ways and as a consequence of this reshape and rebuild aspects of it so that she becomes even more effective in her work (Principle 10). Her account also shows evidence of two of the main types of reflection presented in Chapter 2 namely *descriptive* and *perceptive reflection-on-practice*.

Later in her account Teresa explains how reflection on her teaching is helped by wearing different spectacles. She gives her spectacles different names because they do different things for her. There are for example her 'painful questions specs' that she uses to ask herself reflective questions such as 'What am I doing there?', 'Why am I doing it that way?' and 'How did it come to be like that?' She uses these glasses when she confronts herself and her own teaching. Then there are what she calls her 'professional values specs'. When she sees what she is doing with these on she is looking particularly at the way she is trying to put her values into practice. Questions of value arise in almost every educational decision that we make. Our professional values then make us the kind of teacher that we are. They help us answer the questions, 'What kind of teacher am I?' or 'What kind of teacher do I want to be?'

If you have experience of teaching children with profound and multiple learning difficulties, or if children with special educational needs are being included in your 'mainstream' school, you may empathise with Teresa's values. But because values are a very personal thing you should not be surprised to find that different teachers have different values and that they hold these for certain reasons. It is unwise to assume that, just because a school staff work together, they share the same underlying values. The fact that they are different people with different backgrounds, expectations and career aspirations means that they may see the purposes of education as fulfilling different needs. Teachers have different perspectives on the purposes and processes of education. They therefore have different priorities which leads to differences in values. The same can be said for each school, Local Education Authority and different Governments. Expressing our values is one thing; the way values are perceived, interpreted and actioned by individual teachers and schools is something else. Haydon (1997) puts this point well when he says, 'the difficulty often faced by teachers lies not in outlining the values which a school stands for, but in recognising precisely what this endorsement will mean in practice, particularly if some of the values do not sit comfortably together' (Haydon 1997: 11). An additional challenge for teachers is justifying particular values as being appropriate, ethical, moral and professional given the context in which they work.

So what do you do?

Creating descriptions of our teaching fulfils two fundamental purposes. First it creates a 'text' that we can interrogate by reflecting on it. Reflection has the power to change something that we might not fully understand or have control and influence over, into something with more personal clarity, coherence and meaning. Secondly, the descriptions provide us with evidence of the values which form a rationale for our teaching. Most of us need some help to come to know our teaching in new and more meaningful ways. There are many reflective strategies and techniques available to us which we shall discuss in detail in the next chapter. One useful approach worth mentioning here is described by Boud *et al.* (1985). Their approach to learning through reflection-on-practice begins with a description of a teaching incident. This is followed by a series of steps which are designed to help us enhance our future practice. To get the most from their approach we need to understand four key ideas around which the learning process coheres. These are:

- *Association*, making links between the ideas and feelings we have about the teaching incident we are describing.
- *Integration*, making sense of these associations in some way.
- *Validation*, trying out these new ways of seeing and understanding teaching
- *Appropriation*, taking on board and retaining ownership of these new insights and learning so that we can use them to inform our future teaching.

Boud *et al.* state that practice can be explored by following these six steps:

1. Making a clear, succinct *description* of an incident from your teaching. What to describe is always a tricky issue. Finding something professionally significant is the important thing. It does not have to be something in your practice that 'went wrong'! This step is about *returning to the experience*.
2. Giving an indication of how you felt about the incident and the *feelings* of any others involved (e.g. children, other staff, classroom assistants) as far as you are aware of them and can express them. This step is about *attending to feelings*.
3. Trying to make some sense of what you did and how you felt about it by *connecting* this incident to your previous knowledge and experience of similar incidents. This is about *associations*.

4. Being aware of any new teaching *ideas, insights or changes in values* that may be emerging as a consequence of linking and synthesising aspects of this incident with your previous knowledge and teaching experience. This is about *integration*.
5. *Testing out* your new ideas. Develop an appropriate action plan (e.g. lesson plan, units or schemes of work) and try to improve your teaching by putting your new insights into practice. This step is to do with the *process of validation*.
6. *Integrating and securing* your new ideas and insights into your practice so that they may serve to guide and give added justification to your future teaching. This step is about *appropriation*.

Boud *et al.* (1985) serve to remind us that knowing our practice is centrally about learning to reflect upon it and that this process of reflection involves both looking back (returning to experience) and looking forwards. This means using our new understandings and appreciations to improve our future teaching. This is a most important point, as reflection is often caricatured as only a backward-looking process. Reflection-on-practice gives rise to many consequences. One of these is to inform and improve future action. Implicit in this statement, of course, is the assumption that we have a degree of control and ownership over what we do in school.

But what we do is principally influenced by three things. First, and most fundamentally, by our developing *sense of self*. This is made up of our personal histories of joys, achievements, sadnesses as well as our future intentions and ambitions. Reflection of the kind we describe in this book emphasises the centrality of professional experience in the process of 'understanding the self'. As teachers we experience the world of school through our own particular forms of consciousness. Often 'we are conscious not only of a world about us but also of a world within of inner thoughts, feelings and reflections' (Stevens 1996: 18). Reflection-on-practice does require us to remember things. Through reflective journal writing, critical-incident work, listening to audiotapes of ourselves and watching videos of our classroom teaching for example, our remembering becomes something that we can re-experience and re-see. These and other ways of re-experiencing help us to look for patterns and consistencies as we strive to make sense of our experiences as teachers. 'Thus our conscious awareness is constituted and influenced by our cognitions, by our ways of thinking (as well as feeling). So we attribute meanings to events and responsibility for actions' (Stevens 1996: 19). We are arguing that reflection-on-practice should have a consequence and that it can and should be seen as much more than private contemplation and 'navel-gazing'. A way of putting this is that reflection should help us to do things, to initiate new and better actions and events. This process is often referred to as 'agency'. Reflection can help us develop a sense of agency. One consequence of this is that we are more likely as teachers to hold ourselves and each other responsible for the actions we have or appear to have chosen to do. Reflection then encourages us to account for our actions (if only in our mind) and to give reasons for why we acted as we did.

Secondly, we are affected by *internal school influences* particularly the pressures and opportunities which coalesce to form visions for the future and ways of achieving them. For example, each school's brochure or prospectus creates both a picture of school life and contains a vision of what the school claims is worthwhile education. However these are constructed and communicated, they require us to locate or situate ourselves and our practice within them.

Thirdly, we are influenced by *external agencies*, organisations, networks, associations, unions and Governments who formulate guidelines, frameworks and policies aimed at enhancing the quality of education through school improvements. So to the two questions we raised earlier namely 'What kind of teacher am I?' and 'What kind of teacher do I want to be?' we can add a third and more provocative one, 'What kind of teacher am I forced to be?'

The nature of professional values

'Values' is a contentious word in education. Some simply believe that it suggests that the worth of anything derives from someone or other choosing it. This is only a very partial view (Totterdell 1997). For us, an educational value is something which is socially constructed, consciously and critically reflected upon, discussed and reflected in our feelings, thoughts and actions with our children and colleagues. In this sense, our view of values shares many of the attributes of what Carr (1992) calls 'principled preferences'. He argues that these are of 'quite considerable importance' and that 'unlike other sorts of preferences which are based merely on personal taste or natural disposition, values are standardly a consequence of something approaching intelligent deliberation and are thus, in principle, susceptible of rational appraisal and re-appraisal.' (Carr 1992: 244). Teachers have to make choices every minute of their working day. Every choice implies an underlying value, a 'because', an 'ought' and so on. This makes teachers valuing beings and education a value-laden enterprise.

Values are everywhere. Hardly anyone will say that values do not matter (Ashton 1997: 2). But they do not float around in some kind of void. Neither do they 'grow on trees or fall like manna from heaven, or just look after themselves. On the contrary, they are always vulnerable to the darker side of human nature such as selfishness, greed, self-deception, vanity, lust and cowardice' (Carey 1997: 2). Values are located historically, socially, culturally and politically. They are in what we say or choose not to say, in what we do and do not do. When teachers insist on precision and accuracy in children's work, or praise their use of imagination, censure racist or sexist language, encourage them to show initiative, or respond with interest, patience or frustration to their ideas, children are being introduced to values and value-laden issues (Jackson *et al.* 1993). Values can be heard and read about in school documents, in those from OFSTED, the Teacher Training Agency, the Qualifications and Curriculum Authority, the Department for Education and Employment, Government Ministers and so on. For example when Prime Minister Tony Blair took up office in May 1997, he espoused a commitment to 'decent values' (Runnymede Bulletin 1997). In general this commitment embraced notions of compassion, social justice, liberty, fighting poverty and inequality and so on. With regard to education the White Paper *Excellence in Schools* (Great Britain 1997) set out the way the Government valued 'equality of opportunity', 'high standards for all' and the way society should 'value our teachers'. Further, values can bind people together and give them a sense of belonging, shared commitment and understandings that are central to a collective sense of the moral purposes of education and accountability. But they can also serve to disunite them and highlight differences between them.

> The expectations of interested parties are thus often in conflict, and schools sometimes become the battleground where groups with different value priorities vie for influence and domination ... The values of schools are apparent in their organisation, curriculum and discipline procedures as well as in the relationships between teachers and pupils.
>
> (Halstead and Taylor 1996: 3)

Differences can lead to conflict, but this does not necessarily have to be destructive. Differences in values can be resolved in school but it takes will, determination, an openness and receptiveness to other points of view and perhaps compromise. But, 'the way in which we see our own values and the kind of significance they have for us will affect our attitude towards compromise' (Haydon 1997: 53). It is important though to appreciate that we can feel threatened and vulnerable when our values clash with those of others. The resolution of conflicts that arise from teachers' different value stances is a fundamental task when, for example, groups are working to plan curriculum policy (Johnston 1988). Values can give us a shared language and yet can be used to illustrate how difficult it is at times to be heard and understood by others. For example, alongside these Labour Party Government values run values couched in another discourse, namely that of the marketplace. In this scenario it is the 'market', occupied by providers and consumers, which decides which values are important and should be upheld (Elliott 1994). In this scenario the market forces of efficiency, effectiveness and economy 'rule OK'. A market culture within education suggests the centrality of three key values, namely those to do with rights, choice and accountability.

Parents' rights vis-à-vis the educational establishment are strengthened through membership of school governing bodies ... The language of rights is also prominent in the way the State compels schools to provide parents with more information ... Education reform has also lifted restrictions on enrolment and opened up possibilities for parents to send their children to schools outside their catchment area ... parents are now supposed to be in a position to make informed choices on where to send their children. Finally ... the imperative of the market which forces schools to market themselves ... and the intimidating pressures of the inspection process, suggests that schools are much more accountable to parents.

(Wyness and Silcock 1997: 3)

This 'values discourse' (or language of education) contains reference to inputs and outputs, audits, league tables, value addedness, target setting, performance indicators, delivery of curriculums and benchmarking. All this has amounted to what has been called the 'commodification of education'. It is a values discourse of corporate management. Using the commodity metaphor, new children to a school, for example, are 'raw materials'. 'Batch processesing' generates efficiency and economies of scale. As the quality of the raw material cannot be guaranteed, then the 'factory', to extend the metaphor, has to invest in the processes of selection and standardisation (Curran 1997). This is a powerful image and one that some teachers might object to quite strongly, particularly if they espouse other values. For example Hill (1997) describes 'neo-conservative' values which are quite contrary to those above with their wish to restore a culture of 'back to basics' and their emphasis on traditional values such as respect for authority. Values may also be relatively fixed and reasonably longlasting or much more transient and like fashion and Top Ten records, come and go according to interests and attitudes of the moment.

Teaching is however a profession of values and these values are fundamental to understanding ourselves as teachers, how we relate to others and discharge our role competently and ethically (Scott *et al.* 1993). We believe that it is important to reflect on our values in the light of growing cultural diversity, a widening gulf between the values of imposed educational reform and teacher, self-generated improvement and increased media attention being given in the UK to New Labour's determination to uphold certain values. If values in society in general are controversial then it is not surprising that values in education are anything other than slippery and contestable things also. Halstead and Taylor (1996) encourage us to examine the links between values and education by asking ourselves questions such as:

1. Is there a distinction to be made between private and public values?
2. Do particular values (whether political, aesthetic, moral or religious) have validity only within particular cultures and traditions?
3. Are there overarching principles by which conflicts between values may be resolved?
4. Is there a sufficient basis of shared values in our society to support a common framework of education for all children, or should parents be free to choose between schools and different sets of values?
5. Do the values which are currently taught in schools necessarily reinforce (intentionally or otherwise) the privileged position of certain social classes or religious or cultural groups?
6. Are there any absolute values, or merely changing and relative ones?
7. Should schools reflect traditional values or seek to transform these?
8. Should schools instil values in pupils or teach them to explore and develop their own values?
9. Should teachers aim for a neutral (or value-free) approach to their subject matter? (Halstead and Taylor 1996: 4–5).

In trying to take a firm hold on the nature of values it is important to question three of the common assumptions that we make about them, namely that:

- values are something that come from within us
- values are contested
- there is a relationship between values and practice.

How far do values come from within us?

If, for example, you hold values that have something to do with encouraging children to be responsible for their own actions, to be truthful and considerate towards others, or with developing for your children a just, fair and democratic learning milieu, then you might usefully ask yourself the following questions. How far:

1. did I choose values like these freely?
2. were these values of mine chosen from a set of alternative values?
3. am I able to articulate the consequences for myself and my children of holding these values?
4. are these values that I care passionately about?
5. are these values publically affirmed and supported in school by my colleagues, significant others and children?
6. do I try to live out these values in my daily teaching?
7. do I 'hang on in there' and not let these values go, or compromise on them when faced with difficulties living them out?

Our responses to questions such as these will generate certain kinds of knowledge. It might be practical knowledge grounded in our teaching realities, associated with our past experiences, professionally and politically appropriate or astute, linked to liberal or moral values, an ethical standpoint, associated with notions of lifelong learning or vocational preparation. But one of the most problematic areas in the field of improving teaching is linked to the question, 'So what kinds of knowledge are worth knowing if we wish to improve what we do?' (Lewis 1993). It was Polanyi (1962) who said that only by expressing our tacit knowledge can we ever hope to subject it to some analysis, and through scrutiny, erect a justification for it. In line with this we believe that one important kind of knowledge worth knowing is what we shall call 'values-based knowledge'. This is knowledge that is not just linked to teaching but also tied inextricably to, and derived from, that practice. Values-based knowledge has the power to inform and constantly transform practice. The problem is that often we do not know the values we have. Goldhammer (1966) expresses this well.

> The vast majority ... of values and assumptions from which our ... professional behaviour is governed are implicit. They're inarticulate, they're nebulous, they're buried someplace in our guts and they're not always very accessible ... We can't always rationalise exactly what we're doing ... We can't always make explicit the justifications for the acts we perpetrate ... Only after these things have been made explicit, have been brought to the point where you can enunciate the damn things, can we begin to value those that seem to have some ... integrity and disregard those that seem to be inane.
>
> (Goldhammer 1966: 49)

What are your own values?

We felt that it would be inappropriate in a book such as this and a chapter that focuses on values if we, the authors, did not do what we were advocating. It seemed a contradiction to us. (We shall return to the notion of contradiction shortly.) In other words, we are saying that expressing and justifying our values is a good thing to do but we are not doing it ourselves. We feel this way because we are building an argument that is trying to pursuade you to set out and explain your values and arguing that this is the bedrock upon which reflection-on-practice rests. We are also saying that the reflective process needs to explore the extent to which we are able to live out our values in our everyday teaching. We are suggesting that this process is the catalyst for improving practice.

Some excellent examples of how we might articulate our values are contained in the work of the Kingston Hill Action Research Group (Lomax and Selley 1996) and in an book edited by Lomax (1996) where, in Chapter 1, Lomax *et al.* set out their values in relation to the issue of what constitutes good quality educational research (Lomax *et al.* 1996) In the Lomax and Selley publication a four-part 'enabling framework' is used. For example, Lomax (see below) uses it to show how she claims to have developed and supported the Kingston Hill Action Research Network. (For a full account of action research and its links with reflection-on-practice, see Chapter 4). The Kingston Hill framework contains:

Explaining my values: e.g. 'I care that individuals have open access to higher education and that no one is left outside "to rub their noses against the window".'

Describing my actions: e.g. 'I have encouraged students and their tutors to present their action research at national and international conferences and this has had a practical impact on gaining acceptance for the idea that research should be the basis of teaching and managing in education.'

Explaining the steps I have taken to ensure the appropriateness of my actions: e.g. 'I reflect upon my actions in terms of my values which provide the main criteria against which I judge myself.'

Evidence of how my actions have led to the achievement of my purposes: e.g. 'My own writing which makes explicit my values and provides authentic accounts of my own learning that can be understood by others.'

(Lomax and Selley 1996: 3–4)

We want to offer you an alternative way and one that we believe is highly appropriate also for beginning teachers. It really embraces the first two parts of the framework above. It is intended to encourage you to think carefully about both the content and the form of your value statement. Value statements, in our view, should be personally or collectively meaningful, understandable to others and enable evidence to be gathered to help us to appreciate how far we live the value out in our teaching and general professional lives. Our suggestion is that a value statement needs to be in two parts. It begins with the phrase 'I believe ...'. This is followed by the use of the word, 'because ...'. The first half of the statement is concerned with the 'what', while the second half focuses on 'why', or the rationale for the 'what'. There is no need to be a slave to this structure; it is simply provided to help you to express what you might consider to be your 'core values'. Remember these are the things you really care for and are passionate about. They are the things you want to hold on to. They make you who you are. Some of our core values in our work with teachers and student teachers are thus:

'We believe;
- that it is important for us to try to enable others to think and talk about their values because values give teaching its shape, form and purpose;
- that reflection is at the heart of the learning process because without reflecting systematically and rigorously on what we do how can we ever learn from what we have just done?
- that we encourage others to represent what it is they claim to know in courageous, understandable and imaginative ways because in this way their work might have a positive impact on practice and foster improvement;
- that our teaching and writing should help to give others the means of critical understanding and access to new possibilities because without this we may be constrained and imprisoned by the values, diktats and whims of others;
- in trying to promote educative research with others which is dialogical and which emphasises the question-posing process that helps us to reveal the contradictions in our work and through dialogue, come to some mutual understanding about how practice might be moved forward.'

Value statements are everywhere in education. Some of them do indeed come from within us but some also come from elsewhere. For example if we go back to the 1988 Education Reform Act we find that schools were required to provide a broad and balanced curriculum. The value position was clear. Schools were to prepare young people for 'the opportunities, responsibilities and experiences of adult life' (Great Britain 1988). At that time just exactly what these qualities and values might be were left undefined.

In setting out what makes a successful primary teacher the Teacher Training Agency speak in terms of 'an accomplished communicator and administrator' someone who is 'creative, energetic, enthusiastic, sensible' and with 'a good sense of humour' (TTA 1996/97). They make their values explicit when stressing that it is 'vital to create the correct climate for teaching and learning' and that successful primary teachers will 'need to strike the right balance to allow freedom of expression and creative thought, while maintaining the necessary discipline' (TTA 1996/97: 5). These are the qualities they value in primary teachers. But these qualities have to be nourished during our professional lives. This nourishment often comes in the form of in-service training. In a recent TTA paper (November 1997) called *Invitation to bid for TTA Inset Funds* what is valued as an appropriate bid from institutions of Higher Education for future in-service teacher training is clearly stated. For example, the TTA values INSET that leads to 'the improvement of pupils' performance through the improvement of school teachers' or headteachers' professional knowledge, understanding and skills and their effectiveness in their teaching and/or leadership and management' (TTA 1997a: 3).

Another important source of values came from the School Curriculum and Assessment Authority (SCAA 1996). For example from their paper on values in education and the community we find these statements:

THE SELF: We value each person as a unique being of intrinsic worth, with potential for spiritual, moral, intellectual and physical development and change.

RELATIONSHIPS: We value others for themselves, not for what they have or what they can do for us, and we value these relationships as fundamental to our development and the good of the community.

SOCIETY: We value truth, human rights, the law, justice and collective endeavour for the common good of society. In particular we value families as sources of love and support for all their members, and as a basis of a society in which people care for others.

THE ENVIRONMENT: We value the natural world as a source of wonder and inspiration, and accept our duty to maintain a sustainable environment for the future.

(SCAA 1996: 3–4)

How far are values contested?

In our work with many teachers, almost all have had to address a particularly pervasive value namely, 'that which can be quantified and measured is what is deemed to be important and worthwhile to know'. If we reflect on this example it usefully serves to raise a number of fundamental problems for us to address. These problems are some of the things which tend to make values contestable. First, there is the problem of which values? Secondly, there is the problem of which values have more legitimacy and authority? By this we mean which ones are more appropriate and in what contexts? The first two problems point up the distinction we should make between 'what the values are' and 'what they should or might be'. These are different issues. Thirdly, there is the problem of knowing how to reconcile differences between values. In the context of a school it is the issue of knowing what to do when colleagues either do not appreciate, or wish to subscribe to, a particular value or values. We believe that it is important for teachers to reflect on the nature of their value disagreements. Finally, there is the problem of how we might most competently and ethically live out our values in our teaching and practitioner research?

We subscribe to the view that values are social constructs created and evolving in relation to particular social conditions. Some have argued that:

> ... they are not inherently innate and homogeneous and do not necessarily reflect consensus in a given socio-historical situation. Values are only meaningful in the context of the political and social space from which they emerge. As societies change, so too do their values.
>
> (Ratuva 1997: 1–2)

Some believe that common values may well be something of an aspiration rather than a reality in a culturally pluralistic world. An important point in this argument is that commonality is marred by the inequalities which exist in society and in the domination or subordination of different groups (Morrison 1997). Some dominant individuals or groups in education also have the power to impose meanings and values on others. This kind of impositon of 'alien' values on teachers and their work can lead to conflict or the reproduction of values which prop up and legitimise the dominant group (Gramsci 1971, Bourdieu 1994). Alternatively, others argue that common values need to be sought out and agreed and that these shared values need not be bland, obvious or uninteresting. An important part in this argument is that individual and collective liberty requires and rests on a common set of moral values.

> Without values such as trust, honesty, consideration for other people, love of justice and peace, there can be no liberty, because there can be no orderly society within which individuals can grow and express themselves in interdependence with others.
>
> (Carey 1997: 3)

The argument here about common values is one that does not support the view that they somehow have to be anaemic and bland. They need illustration and contextualising to bring them to life and need to be debated and defended with passion as well as reason, just like our own personal teaching values lived out with our own class of children.

When articulating our individual or whole-school values Prilleltensky and Fox (1997) suggest three things. First, that we try to advance our values in a 'balanced' manner. They say this because they believe that we are prone to over-emphasise one value at the expense of others. In schools we might be accused of over-emphasising self-determination, autonomy and independence which includes a focus on the individual child, while values such as collegiality and collaboration are under-emphasised. Secondly, they suggest that our particular collection, list or configuration of values needs to be fluid and responsive to change. Values should provide a vision of what is good, just and educational at school. They should not be a ball and chain around our feet, but need to be constantly reviewed in the light of changing circumstances. The remnants of old lists of values should not hinder the creation of new ones that form the basis of improved educational practices. Thirdly, they suggest that certain values have more potential for transforming society than others. This is a very important point. For example, caring and compassion may be important values that give our teaching with young children its shape, form and purpose. But living these out in relation to individual pupils may not be enough to change the culture of a school which undermines these values by promoting competition.

What is the relationship between values and practice?

Some professionals in education, teachers and schools argue that a certain set of core values gives them their sense of identity, purpose and integrity. This point is made by Thompson when she argues, 'A shared understanding and appreciation of a profession's values and ethical responsibilities are central to the profession of teaching as they are to other professions' (Thompson 1997: 1). She goes on to say why a Code of Ethics, which she describes as 'a statement of fundamental values and broad ethical principles' is important for the teaching profession. The reasons she lists are these:

- They would serve to help society to judge the integrity of the relationship between the teaching profession and children.
- Without such a Code teachers would work on influential but individual 'educational platforms'.
- It would demonstrate that teaching is fundamentally a moral enterprise.
- It would enable professional values to be reviewed and revised in the light of changes and developments in education and society.
- It would help to raise the profession's morale, raise its self-confidence, sense of purpose and commitment and adjust its expectations, thus improving professional standards (Thompson 1997: 2).

However, some would argue that it is unlikely that one single list of values suits everyone, particularly in a culturally plural society. This issue of common or core values is one central point of discussion in the values debate. Another focuses on the difficulties which arise when we try to implement them or 'live our values out in our teaching'.

In working this through, teachers might be helped by Schein's three professional states which describe different relationships between values and actions (Schein 1969). The states are:

1. *Dynamic stability*, where there is felt to be a congruency between stated or espoused values and values in action.
2. *Precarious stability*, in which we are aware that we are not able to live our values out fully in our practice. This is a state where we are trying to make some adjustments in values and/or practice.
3. *Instability*, in which values and actions are clearly incongruent and where we are not bothering, or are unable, and feel powerless, to take steps to try to live our values out, more fully, in our teaching.

You may feel that in the course of a working week you oscillate between all three states! We believe however that a powerful and significant contribution to this debate about the links between values and practice in the last decade has come from Whitehead (1985, 1989, 1992, 1993, 1996, 1997). The fulcrum of Whitehead's contribution to educational knowledge is the way he encourages us to account for our own educational development through the creation of our own 'living educational theories'. While not denying the value of alternative forms of understanding, he argues that educational theory should be in a living form containing descriptions and explanations of our own development and in so doing acknowledging the context in which the living theory is being produced. He argues that the explanations given by teachers in trying to make sense of their practice come about from addressing, in a serious and critically reflective manner, questions such as 'How do I improve my practice here?' Living theory then is educational theory based on educational practice as lived and experienced by teachers them-selves. These theories are 'claims to know' which, like all kinds of theory, have to be able to respond to questions of validity. This means that we have to have some standards or criteria that we understand and can use in order to test the validity of a teacher's claim to know their own educational development. In its most straightforward form the issue of validity is reflected in the question, 'How do I/we know that what the teacher says about their own educational development and practice, is true?'

> A living theory is one that is continuously created and recreated through the validated explanations that individual managers offer of their own practices as they pursue their educational goals. These explanations are stimulated by intentional, committed action that stems from practical concerns about managing, and are reached through the analysis of careful descriptions that depend on rigorous methods of data collection and analysis.
>
> (Lomax *et al*. 1996: 16)

At this point we want to draw your attention to the way living theory helps us to understand the links between values and action. Living educational theory coheres around notions:

- that teaching is a value-laden activity
- of the living 'I'
- of the self existing as a living contradiction.

With regard to the first notion Whitehead states, 'I think values are embodied in our practice and their meanings can be communicated in the course of their emergence in practice' (White-head 1992: 193). He also argues that values offer explanations for our actions. The notion of the living 'I' is contained in the action-questions that characterise enquiries that seek to develop this form of knowledge. Questions such as, 'How do I improve my teaching?', 'How do I improve this process of education here?' and 'How do I live my values more fully in my practice?'. This living 'I' is such a potent idea and relevant to the kinds of reflection-on-practice that we are advocating here. The living 'I' arises, in our view, in part, from the way we act within and upon the world. It derives also from an awareness of the 'me', namely an image of the kind of teacher that we are. The living 'I' can be seen then as a fusion of what we might call 'personal' and 'social' identities. Our individuality as a teacher is expressed through the values we place on the different experiences and things that make up our professional world. The living 'I' we believe is nourished by our abilty to be reflective, to stand back and acknowledge the potential we have to improve how things are in our teaching. The living 'I' lives in the worlds of the actual, possible and the desirable.

The final notion of 'I' existing as a living contradiction in the creation of living educational theory is appealing and liberating. Whitehead puts it this way.

> ... think about how you have tried to overcome problems in your professional practice. I think such a reflection will reveal that you have experienced a tension in holding certain values and experiencing their negation at the same time in your practice.
>
> (Whitehead 1992: 6)

Put simply, this means as a teacher we often say we value something, for example facilitating pupil discussion, and then do the opposite, we dominate the classroom discourse. We talk too much! Here we exist as a living contradiction. When I say that I want to give all my children an equal amount of time and then I find myself concentrating on those who demand more of my attention, I am denying my values in my practice. Again I am a living contradiction. We can view the contradictions within our teaching as professional growth points: tensions that need to be reflected upon. Sometimes we feel a sense of powerlessness when appreciating the fact that we hold certain values while at the same time experiencing their denial in our practice. Sometimes, through reflection, we develop new appreciations about what is possible and where improvements can most usefully be targeted. Sometimes we just have to say to ourselves 'Well, that's how it is here right now and there isn't a great deal I can do about things for the time being.' It is too simplistic to think that practice moves smoothly and unproblematically from values being negated in practice to a position where we do live them out. Moving forward and developing our practice may involve some kind of creative synthesis of previous contradictions. This view of practice, which has the notion of a contradiction at its heart is a 'tensioned' one and is called a 'dialectical' view. If we hold this view we aim to develop our insights and understandings through a process of posing questions and trying to answer them.

Moving our thinking and practice forward is fundamentally about understanding the links between our values and our teaching. The nature and educative potency of our values needs to be seen in relation to our practice: our values emerge through our practice. Our teaching reflects our values-in-action. As we accept responsibility for the education of our children so we need to accept responsibility for making sincere, transparent, systematic and convincing efforts to try to live our values out as fully as possible in our teaching. The ways we might do this and the role of reflection in the process is the subject of the next chapter.

CHAPTER FOUR

Reflection-on-practice: Resolving Teaching Concerns

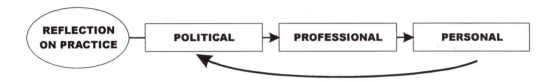

In the last chapter we said that one of the best ways to characterise teaching was through the values that permeate it and give it its direction and purpose. Teaching children is the act through which values come alive. By watching the interactions between teachers and their children, we should be able to infer the teacher's values. Values help the teacher to make decisions on how to proceed. But there is something else which is central to this process of making wise, creative and professional decisions, and that is evidence. Confident and competent teaching requires teachers to reflect systematically and rigorously on evidence derived from practice. Evidence comes in many forms: it can be formal and publically available evidence such as OFSTED reports, National Curriculum SAT scores, the school's performance in the form of league tables and school brochures. Then there is formal but relatively less available evidence like minutes of School Governor's meetings, school policy statements and teachers' schemes of work. There is also evidence that teachers might gather on children's learning and their own teaching. All this evidence can be collected in different ways, by different people, at different times, with certain interests and audiences to serve in mind. It can, for example, be gathered through observation, discussion and conversation, tape and video recording. Evidence can also be analysed in a variety of ways and presented to highlight issues, themes, trends, tensions, accomplishments, areas for concern and action. Reflective teaching and learning then is evidence-based. To understand this more fully we need to explore the links between teaching, evidence and reflection.

There are three important sources of influence that serve to illustrate the nature and importance of the links between teaching, evidence and reflection. These are the political, professional and the personal. We shall illustrate each one with reference to the induction of new teachers, the teacher-as-researcher movement and a personal commitment to compiling a development profile.

The political: the induction of new teachers

In the recent Government consultation document (DfEE 1998a) *Induction of New Teachers* the links between teaching, evidence and reflection are set out. For example,

> We will establish a new national framework which will give every new teacher a clear statement of what is expected of them; a guarantee of the necessary support and guidance to meet those expectations; sufficient time and space to reflect on and develop their performance; and opportunities to exchange experiences with other teachers, both others new to the profession and those already in schools, and, above all, the chance to learn from observing the best, experienced teachers at work.
>
> (DfEE 1998a: 3)

Reflection is explicitly mentioned. Without systematic reflection-on-practice how is the new teacher able to develop their performance? Evidence in the form of observations of practice will create the chance to learn if the new teacher reflects on this evidence in a creative and critically reflective manner. Later in the document we find, 'From May this year (1998), for the first time, all students completing teacher training courses will have a Career Entry Profile, which will summarise the new teacher's particular strengths and priorities for their further professional development' (p. 8). In the same paragraph 10 the phrase 'record agreed targets and an action plan for their achievement' is used and in the following paragraph we find that the new teacher should 'observe and learn from the best existing practice'. In Section 6, which is about an effective programme of support, the Government sets out an impressive list of key elements. Pertinent to this discussion is element 3 and 'regular observation of teaching and feedback', element 4 and 'regular discussions ... to review professional practice ... and update the action plan' and element 7 which states that new teachers will 'have their work observed and commented on by the Headteacher and access to the Headteacher to discuss any additional training needs or difficulties they may be experiencing' (pp.9–10).

In Section 8 on the standards required to be met by new teachers, we find another statement which links teaching with evidence and reflection. The final standard 13 states that teachers must, when assessed, demonstrate that they 'can take responsibility for their own future professional development and keep up to date with research and developments in pedagogy and in the subject(s) they teach' (para. 22). In assessing the new teacher against the standards a wide range of evidence will be relevant. Six forms of evidence are identified. These are:

- a written report from the line manager, drawing on formative assessment that has taken place throughout the year;
- where the line manager is not the Head, an interview between the new teacher and the Head to review progress;
- any reports from any mentor teachers or other external trainers or from schools who may have contributed to the new teacher's programme;
- evidence of achievement of pupils for whom the new teacher has particular responsibility;
- the Career Entry Profile; and
- any judgements of the new teacher's performance by OFSTED inspectors (para. 29).

The consultation document gives us much to think about. For example, for those involved in initial teacher training emphasis will need to be given on helping students with needs and wants analysis, and knowing the difference, on action learning (McGill and Beaty 1996) and action research. Target setting which is realistic, appropriate and in harmony with the context in which the student or new teacher is working will also be important. Targets also have to be meaningful. Students as well as new teachers will need to be helped to distinguish between those targets that have some kind of personal meaning for them, meaning for their children and for others in the school. Targets are set for different reasons and serve different ends. Clarity will be needed to sort out targets, as ends, and the most appropriate means to achieve them. Not only this, but the purposes behind the setting of one target rather than another will need to be articulated.

Evidence in the form of observations of practice is also a prominent part of the consultation document. Making observations of practice has been a central feature of the teaching profession for many years with the ORACLE project (Observation Research and Classroom Learning Evaluation) being the most extensive piece of classroom observation research in the UK to date. One of the aims of the project was to describe, 'some of the richness and variety of what goes on in a modern Primary classroom' and 'to search for patterns from among those events in order to help explain why certain teachers do one thing while others do something else' (Galton *et al.* 1980: 4). The lessons learnt from this major project and the critiques of it (Scarth and Hammersley 1993) seem very pertinent, given the exposure that observational evidence receives in the consultation paper. What is observed, how, when, in what ways and with what purposes in mind, are enduring questions. In the document a number of different 'observers' are identified like the new teacher's line manager, mentor, headteacher and OFSTED inspectors. All these people are likely to have different kinds of experience and abilities to observe. They are also likely to have their own agendas and perhaps conflicting ones. Even if they are working to some kind of common goal, the settings in which the observations are undertaken, that is teaching and non-teaching (DfEE 1998a: para. 30) will make the formulation of assessment that follows a 'nationally-agreed format' a challenging business.

Feedback is also 'talked-up' in the document, be it in relation to revising action plans, in the guise of 'discussions' with the new teacher's line manager or through the 'interview' process with the headteacher. Feedback, like observation, is another conventional plank upon which professional development is traditionally facilitated. Important distinctions will need to be made between confirmatory and corrective feedback. The former is feedback where the new teacher gets to know that they are on course, that things are moving forwards in an acceptable manner, that is, a shared understanding of achievements and agreement about where to exert action in order to enhance practice. Corrective feedback is what it suggests. It is the kind of feedback that focuses on and emphasises changing things with a view to improving the current state of practice. This should not overwhelm the new teacher otherwise it will defeat the purpose of the whole process: corrective does not mean punitive.

To stand a chance of helping to move the new teacher's practice forward, the teacher needs an opportunity to comment on the feedback, to expand upon it and to be helped to discover real ways of doing things differently that are within their compass. Often, in reality, feedback to teachers on their performance contains a bit of both types. The bottom line is that feedback should be in the service of two intentions. First, that it should help teachers to manage their work effectively, competently and ethically by offering new perspectives on things and by opening up unnoticed possibilities and alternatives. Secondly, feedback should help teachers to become better at helping themselves to move their own thinking and practice forward. Providing quality feedback is a skilful business. Those involved in the induction of new teachers will need, not only a repertoire of basic communication skills such as empathy, attending, listening, understanding, probing and summarising, but also some fairly sophisticated and advanced communication skills of which handling resistance and reluctance, helping new teachers to challenge their own teaching and helping them to move from possibilities to making choices, will be essential. Quality feedback is dependent upon making sense of reflections-on-practice, the new teacher's practice. The skilfulness of the new teacher's line manger in this regard is important.

In the final 'standard' number 13 new teachers will have to demonstrate that they are keeping up to date with research. This is placed in the context of taking responsibility for their own professional development and is another hugely complex demand. Some of the central issues here involve the type of research, the new teacher's access to it and its usefulness and impact on practice-in-context. For many new teachers, research is still something rather abstract, 'out there', unrelated to everyday practice and undertaken by 'others' rather than teachers themselves. Time constraints and lack of skills are the often cited reasons for others doing it rather than the teachers themselves.

Research being done by others raises the issue of ownership. If teachers have no stake in the knowledge generated through research, then how can they feel committed to it and believe in it? Teachers also need research that helps them to explain aspects of their everyday practice in their own particular school settings. If you think that research is only about the search for generalisations you may also believe that what is being said applies to all contexts of practice. But what happens when you find that, having put your confidence in this research, the research does not fit, does not work, does not help to explain your practice with your own children? You might try to force-fit it but it still does not help! In this scenario we might need to get access to a different type of research. Some teachers have difficulty in understanding research because of the way the research account is written. To benefit from research, teachers have to be able to understand it. These suspicions, misgivings and stereotypes are still around (Ghaye *et al.* 1996b) But just as there are different types of reflection and evidence that serve different interests, so too are there different types of research, generated in different ways to serve different needs.

In the context of the consultation document, it is likely to be 'educative research' (Gitlin and Russell 1994) which new teachers might find useful. This research has a number of relevant features. For example it:

- encourages the participants in the research to jointly negotiate the meaning of what is being studied;
- acknowledges that what is discovered through the research is embedded in a particular historical and cultural context;
- follows a responsive question-and-answer approach. Formulating an appropriate research question and using questions with which to confront practice is important;
- questions the taken-for-grantedness of everyday practice;
- gives a voice to practitioners themselves as they jointly construct new meanings about practice and question the influences and structures that serve to reinforce and constrain the production of new meanings and alternative ways of doing things;
- views research as a process and not just as a product. Research as a product gets teachers into thinking that research is not grounded in their practice but rather obtained from elsewhere and applied to their practice. Educative research is primarily a process with turning points and critical incidents that redirect the inquiry, that has the power to alter the questions being asked and influence teaching as insights are progressively accumulated;
- places the researcher (the teacher) within the research account. The teacher's views, biases, perspectives and subjectivities which serve to influence the research process and

give the account its form and character make the research authentic;
- changes the traditional view of the terms validity and reliability. Validity is about truthfulness and how far the reader can trust the researcher's account. Reliability is about the extent to which different researchers, using the same procedures, might come to the same conclusions. In educative research 'truthfulness' is arrived at through discussion and the mutual understandings that are derived from listening to and challenging all participant views and positions. The reader needs to have access to the processes that precipitate these constructed and negotiated understandings. Reliability is altered because of the commitment educative research has to develop the voice of the teacher in their own school settings. It is often both undesirable and inappropriate for procedures to remain unchanged from school setting to school setting. What is important is that the procedures are justified in relation to the research question, relevant to the school context and reported in such a way that others can judge how far they have been deployed systematically and rigorously. These characteristics have much in common with action research which we discuss later in this chapter.

The final thing we need to be clear about is what is meant in standard 13 when the Department for Education and Employment say that new teachers need to take responsibility for their own future development. Again we need to articulate some of the links between teaching, evidence and reflection that this poses. One restricted interpretation of this is to say that responsible action is when teachers ask themselves why they are doing what they are doing. Dewey (1933) however had much to say about responsibility in the context of professionl development through reflection; he extends our interpretation. Essentially for him it was about the consequences of the act of teaching and school practices. He regarded responsibility as a characteristic of reflective teaching. Being responsible is being prepared to consider what is worthwhile in the educative relationships teachers have with their children. Responsible action is more than just considering 'what works' for me here, right now and involves a reflection on both the means and ends of education. Issues such as in what ways my teaching benefits my children and its impact on them are addressed, as opposed to questions of the kind, 'How far have my learning objectives been achieved?' Broader issues such as these inevitably draw us into the realms of the politico-economic, socio-cultural, the moral and ethical as we strive to act responsibly (Ashcroft and Griffiths 1989). It draws us into the world beyond the classroom and school and invites the teacher to consider the structures that serve to constrain and curtail responsible action.

Dewey also talked about open-mindedness and wholeheartedness as essential attributes of reflective action. The first is about reflecting on what we do, confronting those things upon which our practice and that of others is predicated and being open to other possibilities. The latter concerns the fundamental mindset and approach of teachers to their work. Wholeheartedness for Dewey is about being energetic and enthusiastic and about approaching teaching in a frame of mind that accepts that there is always something new to be learned from each lesson and working day. In the work of Zeichner and Liston (1996) this responsibility for professional development is clearly linked to reflective practice.

> When embracing the concept of reflective teaching, there is often a commitment by teachers to internalize the disposition and skills to study their teaching and become better at teaching over time, a commitment to take responsibility for their own professional development. This assumption of responsibility is a central feature of the idea of the reflective teacher.
>
> (Zeichner and Liston 1996: 6)

There are many lists of the attributes of the reflective practitioner (Pollard 1996, 1997, Pollard and Triggs 1997) and much debate about their contents. One that is a useful start and which is congruent with much of what we have said thus far, is that advanced by Zeichner and Liston. They argue that a reflective teacher:

- examines, frames and attempts to solve the dilemmas of classroom practice,
- is aware of and questions the assumptions and values he or she brings to teaching,
- is attentive to the institutional and cultural contexts in which he or she teaches,
- takes part in curriculum development and is involved in school change efforts,
- takes responsibility for his or her own professional development.

(Zeichner and Liston 1996: 6)

Some of the important things to note here are the focus on dilemmas in practice, values in a context and the notions of development and change. Eraut (1994a) helps to take us further by arguing that the teacher as a reflective practitioner is based upon the following set of assumptions:

- A teacher needs to have a repertoire of methods for teaching and promoting learning.
- Both selection from this repertoire and adaptation of methods within that repertoire are necessary to best provide for particular pupils in particular circumstances.
- Both the repertoire and this decision-making process within it are learned through experience.
- Teachers continue to learn by reflecting on their experience and assessing the effects of their behaviour and their decisions.
- Both intuitive information gathering and routinised action can be brought under critical control through this reflective process and modified accordingly.
- Planning and pre-instructional decision-making is largely deliberative in nature. There is too little certainty for it to be a wholly logical process.
- These processes are improved when small groups of teachers observe and discuss one another's work.

(Eraut 1994a in Eraut 1995a: 231–2)

Eraut's assumptions intersect with a number of the principles we set out in Chapter 2. For example with Principle 1 and reflective practice being understood as a discourse and Principle 2 with reflection being energised by experience. When the DfEE talks about new teachers being responsible for their own future development they are really making a statement about what it is to be a professional. Eraut (1995a) argues that what makes a reflective practitioner also a professional practitioner is:

- a moral commitment to serve the interests of students by reflecting on their well-being and their progress and deciding how best it can be fostered or promoted;
- a professional obligation to review periodically the nature and effectiveness of one's practice in order to improve the quality of one's management, pedagogy and decision-making;
- a professional obligation to continue to develop one's practical knowledge both by personal reflection and through interaction with others.

(Eraut 1995a: 232)

Taking responsibility for one's own future development is dependent upon the new teacher's ability to reflect on their own practice and that of others. Reflective practice is responsible action. But teacher development through reflection can be undermined. Gore and Zeichner (1995) suggest that this can be done in a number of ways. For example, by devaluing the practical wisdom and theories of teachers and celebrating the knowledge held and generated only by those in the 'academy', and by restricting reflection-on-practice to a consideration of utilitarian and technical issues rather than the moral purposes of education, questions of equity and social justice. In other words by focusing on the 'what' and 'how' of teaching rather than on the reasons and purposes of it. For example, by focusing on the classroom and neglecting to understand that, although immediate, concrete and well-known to the teacher, the classroom is part of a bigger social, political, cultural, economic and historical context. Finally, development through reflection is undermined if teachers see reflection as a solitary and intro-spective activity only, and one where they refer only to their own work. We have argued that reflection can also be collaborative, collegial, discursive and public. Through this process they can 'position' their work and understandings in relation to others. Reflection-on-practice as responsible action in this sense is therefore about collaborative learning, self- and collective re-evaluation of practice.

The professional: the teacher-as-researcher

One of the purposes of reflection is to play its part in the complex process of improving indi-vidual and collective action. It is about helping to move thinking and practice forward. There are many ways to realise these intentions. A fundamental part of the process of improving the quality of action in classrooms and schools is teachers researching their own practice. Personal and collective knowledge about improving teaching and learning develops in and through prac-tice. It develops when teachers study or research their own practices themselves. Reflections on the role of self and the research process as it unfurls in real world settings such as class-rooms, is an explicit and integral characteristic of certain styles of research, such as action research (Ghaye and Wakefield 1993).

The idea of teachers viewing themselves as researchers in their own teaching situation emanates principally from the pioneering work of Lawrence Stenhouse in the late 1960s (Stenhouse 1968, 1975) and the Schools Council Humanities Curriculum Project (1967–72) which he directed. There are many excellent accounts of the profound and lasting impact his work has had on the notions of school-based curriculum development and teachers' profes-sional development (Stenhouse 1980, 1983, Noffke 1997, Elliott 1997). Of particular relevance to this book are his ideas that teachers:

- should regard themselves as researchers and 'best judges of their own practice' (McNiff 1991);
- need to reflect critically and systematically on their practice;
- should have a commitment to question their practice and that this should be the basis for teacher development;
- should have the commitment and the skills to study their own teaching and in so doing develop the art of self-study;
- might benefit from their teaching being observed by others and discussing it with them in

an open and honest manner;
- should have a concern to question and to test theory in practice.

(Stenhouse 1975: 143–4)

In discussing the relationship between theory and practice Carr (1995) refers to Stenhouse thus: 'The relationship between theory and practice ... must be understood in terms of the public sphere rather than the private' (Carr 1995: 15). The Stenhouse view of research as a public activity, as systematic and sustained enquiry, planned and self-critical, which is made public, is an extremely important idea (Stenhouse 1981: 113). He argued that if teachers were to develop their practice and their understandings of theory, they would have to place their research in the public domain where it would be critiqued and perhaps utilised. The process of teacher development was not a private act of private reflections on practice but a public process of one kind or another.

The thrust then of Stenhouse's work is that:

- all teaching ought to be based on research,
- the idea of teachers as researchers supports, nourishes and extends the professionalism of the teacher,
- it is an important element in the professionalisation of teaching, and
- it reinforces the teacher's sense of professional autonomy and responsibility.

For Stenhouse;

> ... curriculum development was synonymous with professional development, and professional development was itself construed as a research process in which teachers systematically reflect on their practice and use the results of this reflection in such a way as to improve their own teaching. By relating this idea of 'teacher as researcher' to an analysis of professionalism, Stenhouse was able to argue that professional development required teachers to be provided with opportunities and resources to study their own practice through systematic reflection and research.
>
> (Carr 1989: 7)

This was being advocated nearly 30 years ago. It is interesting to note that in the DfEE consultation document (DfEE 1998a), discussed earlier in this chapter, the same issues, identified by Stenhouse, of appropriate 'opportunities and resources' are being advocated for the proper induction of new teachers into the profession again in the late 1990s!

Just as action research was an important part of the theory of development which emanated from the Humanities Curriculum Project so too was the recognition that the quality of the teacher's reflective framework was a decisive factor in teacher development (Day 1987). Action research involved the conscious act of reflection on practice. There have been many excellent texts which describe the nature, purposes, processes and impact of action research on teachers' thinking, practice and the context in which teaching and learning takes place (Carr and Kemmis 1986, Kemmis and McTaggart 1988a, 1988b, Henry 1991, Zuber-Skerritt 1996, O'Hanlon 1996, McNiff *et al.* 1996, McKernan 1996, Goodson 1997, Hollingsworth 1997). There have also been numerous action research projects undertaken by individuals and groups which have been written up and disseminated for example through the Classroom (and more recently Collaborative) Action Research Network's (CARN) Bulletins and the international

Journal of Educational Action Research. The experiences of some of the major British-funded action research projects have also been well reviewed (Sarland 1995). In summary, Sarland found that a number of themes and issues emerged from his analysis. These were that action research might usefully be seen to be about:

- the worthwhileness and authenticity of practitioner knowledge;
- practitioners taking control of the ways teaching and learning is understood and of the production of this knowledge;
- the generation of theory in the classroom;
- cycles of action and reflection;
- collaborative ways of working;
- outsiders as facilitators;
- the contribution action research studies make to educational knowledge;
- the process of writing to promote the action researcher's own understanding;
- a belief that action research is best suited to professional and curriculum development.

In a complementary view McNiff *et al*. (1992) argue that action research may be characterised as a way of working that:

- is practitioner generated;
- is workplace oriented;
- seeks to improve something;
- starts from a particular situation;
- adopts a flexible trial and error approach;
- accepts that there are no final answers;
- aims to validate any claims it makes by rigorous justfication processes.

Whitehead (1993) suggests that the improvement process might most usefully begin with a reflection on the negation of values in practice thus:

- I experience a concern when some of my values are denied in my practice.
- I imagine a solution to the concern.
- I act in the direction of the solution.
- I evaluate the solution.
- I modify my practice in the light of the solution.

Action, reflection and resolving teaching concerns

Elements of Sarland, McNiff and Whitehead in particular can be found in the following extract of the work of a First School (5–9 years) teacher called Kay, who is researching her own practice. In appreciating this example we should remember that action research is not monolithic. There is not just one type and there is much debate about its aims and methods. For example, you will find that people write about participatory and collaborative forms of action research. Additionally Carr and Kemmis (1986) distinguished between technical, practical and emancipatory types of it; these are summarised in Zuber-Skerritt (1996). What follows is an example of action research which is both collaborative and practical. Kay has sought and gained the support and participation of her children, school staff, governors and parents. By 'practical' we mean that it shows how the teacher is trying to become more effective in her work and also how she is endeavouring to understand her practice more fully and richly. Kay is engaging in a transformatory process which has the potential to enable her to make wiser, more competent and ethical decisions. She used Whitehead's framework as the basis for an action plan. Her research question was:

How can I use the principles and procedures of action research to improve my teaching of health education and link this to the development of a whole school health education programme?

She posed the following questions and offered a personal response.

Question 1: What is my concern?

'Health education is not coordinated well within my school. There is no policy or even guidelines. Teachers depend upon their own, often limited, knowledge and rarely seek guidance from myself. This suggests to me that a rather complacent attitude exists. Most staff, I think, feel that health education is being taught adequately. From what I see and hear, I strongly believe that this is not the case. My concern is that health education at school should be a relevant and meaningful learning experience for all children. This means that staff have to be informed, confident and enthusiastic about it.'

Question 2: Why am I concerned?

'Health education is an important area for children of this age and one which is not given the attention it deserves. Many aspects of health education are being neglected simply because staff are not aware of them. The National Curriculum Council (1991) suggested nine "topic" areas which should be developed. Similarly various authorities have produced guidelines aimed at improving general public awareness. My belief is that the message is still not being received by staff and children.'

Question 3: What do I think I can do about it?

'My principal aim is to motivate members of staff to recognise the value of health education and to encourage them to incorporate it more frequently into their practice. I also intend to emphasise cross-curricular links and to reassure colleagues that this "additional" subject need not be regarded as "yet another extra in an already overcrowded curriculum", I want them to see it as an extension of aspects of their current good practice.'

Question 4: What kind of 'evidence' can I collect to help me make some judgements about what is happening?

'I believe there to be four crucial steps:
  1. Assessment of my own classroom practice and the extent to which I incorporate health

education in my teaching. At present I know that I do not fully practice what I preach! I do not live out my own educational values and I want to change this but this is not as easy as it seems.

2. Requesting help from colleagues in assessing their own health education values. Although I realise that this could be problematic. I believe it to be very significant to determine how important staff members consider health education to be, bearing in mind individual priorities and the politics within the school. They have got to want to change things. It's then my job to try to give them the skills and courage to do this.

3. Begin looking at the accessibility of resources within the school, paying particular attention to how frequently colleagues request information. This will involve the compilation of a resource guide/list for ease of reference. Resources at the health education centre would also need to be included.

4. Determine how parents and governors regard health education. I will need to involve parents in the study by requesting their views on health education – their fears or concerns. This necessarily involves collaboration with the headteacher and, from experience, I believe that she will be only too willing to assist.'

Question 5: How do I plan to collect such evidence?

'My intention is to work through the following steps (corresponding to those issues identified in question 4):

1. Careful monitoring of my own teaching to include field notes on the amount of time spent on health education and a record of the nature of that teaching.

2. Staff curriculum meetings. These will be both formal and informal, the headteacher having already agreed to give directed time for meetings concerned with curriculum development. This will enable me to tape meetings, supplement my field notes and reflect upon the staff's opinions to plan the next step. It will also mean exposing my own teaching practices and results of my personal investigation which I believe to be a necessary part of the process. I will also prepare guidelines for colleagues based on a simple questionnaire style – yet to be devised. Informal comments will be logged as soon as possible after the event. The importance of this is evident in McNiff's (1991) statement, "Immediate recording of events as they happen will avoid inevitable skewing of the data and give a truer picture of the action and how we interpreted the action" (p. 71).

3. Liaison with the health education department will help me to assess the relevance of resources in school at present. It will involve visits to the health education centre and discussions with the staff there. I have arranged with both my headteacher and the health education department to take time to do this. This will enable me to keep up to date, not only with current trends, but with political initiatives also. A resource library can then be established within the school.

4. Requests for parents and governors to air their views will be carried out in the form of a questionnaire. I appreciate the limitations of a questionnaire, insofar as it is notoriously difficult to get the information desired, but feel that it is a pragmatic response to gain an insight into the *general* feelings of our parents and governors.'

Question 6: 'How shall I check that my judgement about what has happened is reasonably fair and accurate?'

'When first introduced to the notion of a "critical friend" I spoke to a member of staff concerning the possibility of using her honest opinions and advice. She happily agreed to act as a critical friend and would, she said, be prepared to make constructive comments regarding matters of curriculum development.

Similarly, I have already heeded the advice of a college critical friend regarding the focus of my research. We met to discuss each other's proposals and I was able to use his suggestions to re-direct my thinking and to define my plans more clearly. Through discussion with him I realised that I was being too ambitious and needed to "scaledown" the project to concentrate more deeply on the *process* of developing a health education policy, rather than the hurried implementation and evaluation of one. In this way, I can be more thorough in my research and hopefully produce an informed workable document for the school.

I am also fortunate enough to have a supportive headteacher who is prepared to assist me wherever possible during each stage of development. I would hope that all three critical friends will help validate my findings by commenting on my procedures and results.

As I progress from analysing my own classroom practice to involving other members of staff in the policy-making process, I shall use their comments and criticisms to help structure future plans. This will enable me to validate my findings as I progress and hopefully reduce the risk of any misunderstanding. I appreciate the fact that colleagues need to be kept informed of developments throughout the research and have received assurance from them that they will support me during this project. I think my colleagues will judge the worthwhileness of the whole very soon after I expose them to it. I intend to do my best to keep in touch with their thoughts and feelings so as to produce an effective shared policy.

I would also hope to use the children as a source of validation. Since my own classroom practices will be re-structured to a certain extent, the children will be encouraged to make comments regarding the changes. I believe that, at 9 years of age, many are capable of making constructive suggestions and of reflecting upon the work covered. I anticipate that this will be in the form of tape recordings during discussion times and, perhaps, through the use of diaries. I shall, of course, use my own field notes as a source of information and validation.

Finally, I hope to use tutorials at the college where I am studying part-time for a Masters degree to discuss what I am doing and how I am progressing. While I can collaborate with colleagues and children within my workplace, I think it is necessary to liaise with an "outsider" who is involved less directly with the research and who may see matters from a different perspective.

I can but do my best!'

This action plan gave Kay the structure and direction for carrying out her health education improvement agenda. Carr and Kemmis (1986) define much of the character of action research when they say that it is a form of self-reflective enquiry undertaken by participants in social situations in order to improve the rationality and justice of their own practices, their understanding of these practices, and the situations in which the practices are carried out ... In terms of method, a self-reflective spiral of cycles of planning, acting, observing and reflecting is central to the action research approach.

(Carr and Kemmis 1986: 162)

The work of Kemmis and McTaggart (1988a), which evolved from Lewin's earlier work (1946), refer to the spiral of action-and-reflection as the four 'moments' of action research. The same terms are used:

1. *Plan:* Develop a plan of action to improve what is already happening.
2. *Act:* Act to implement the plan.
3. *Observe:* Observe the effects of the action in the context in which it occurs.
4. *Reflect:* Reflect on these as a catalyst for further planning and subsequent action.

Reflection on action involves trying to determine, individually and collectively, what has been learnt from the enquiry process, the consequences of the intervention and the need to re-formulate the teaching concern if necessary.

Action research thus has an individual aspect, action researchers change themselves; and a collective aspect, action researchers work with others to achieve change and to understand what it means to change. That is, action research is concerned simultaneously with changing individuals, on the one hand, and, on the other, the culture of the groups, institutions and communities to which they belong. It is important to emphasise that these changes are not impositions: individuals and groups agree to work together to change themselves, individually and collectively, and to document the nature of, and changes in their work.

(Henry 1993: 60)

Just as there is much debate about the nature and aims of action research so too there is debate about how teachers conduct their enquiries and work to resolve their teaching concerns. For example the 'Teachers as Researchers in the Context of Award Bearing Courses and Research degrees' project in the UK funded by the Economic and Social Research Council, explored the claims made for action research and the criticisms levelled against it (Elliott *et al.* 1996). One of its major findings was that 'a great diversity of approaches (were) exemplified in the dissertations' (p. 14). The main kinds of variation found were summarised thus:

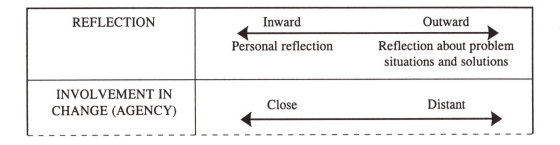

REFLECTION	Inward ⟷ Outward
	Personal reflection — Reflection about problem situations and solutions
INVOLVEMENT IN CHANGE (AGENCY)	Close ⟷ Distant

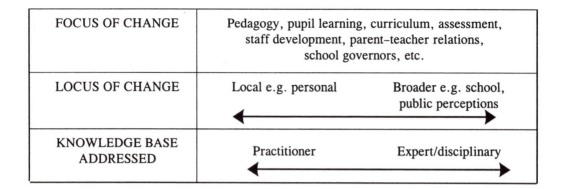

FOCUS OF CHANGE	Pedagogy, pupil learning, curriculum, assessment, staff development, parent–teacher relations, school governors, etc.	
LOCUS OF CHANGE	Local e.g. personal ◄——————————►	Broader e.g. school, public perceptions
KNOWLEDGE BASE ADDRESSED	Practitioner ◄——————————►	Expert/disciplinary

Educational action research and the role of reflection

Diversity of purpose and approach is also a feature of the reflective part of the action–reflection cycle. Reflection is an integral part of action research but there is a lack of clarity about it. Reflection needs to be built into each part of the action research process. In particular we have identified four parts of this process where reflection is crucial. They are in:

- problematising teaching and learning
- observing and creating a 'text' about our work
- confronting ourselves and the teaching context
- refocusing and creative action.

Problematising teaching and learning

- This can involve an element of discomfort, even threat, as we look at ourselves and our working environment. It is far easier to accept our current circumstances and adopt the line of least resistance!
- There is a need to reflect on what you perceive to be the inadequacies of your teaching and also on your strengths and how to nourish and sustain existing good practice.
- It is not mandatory to introduce new and different perspectives from 'outside' but through collective action, to reflect upon the basis (values) on which practice is taking place and to examine the real possibilities which practice, on this occasion, chooses to ignore or cannot enact.
- Problematising teaching and learning means we reflect upon what is happening and why, what our educational intentions are and why we hold them.

'Text' creation

- The process of reflection should generate a 'text'. This is a record and evidential-base derived from practice. One important 'text' is the reflective conversation. Another could be evidence in the form of a learning journal, evidence in a professional portfolio or Career Entry Profile.

- The 'text' then needs to be 'read'. That is to say, through a reflective dialogue, it is opened-up (deconstructed), the different messages are made sense of, and a new text constructed with richer insights and meaning. The emphasis should be on learning from experience and on moving thinking and practice forward in the light of this.
- Conferral and dialogue are essential in this process.

Confronting ourselves and the teaching context

Some key reflective questions that individual teachers might ask themselves are:

- What is my practice like?
- Why is it like this?
- How has it come to be this way?
- What would I like to improve and why?

Additionally through peer observations and collaborative action it is important that the following questions are confronted:
- How far do I live my educational values out in my work?
- How far does the 'culture' of my workplace help or hinder this?

Refocusing and creative action

Reflection needs to have a consequence. One consequence is to strive to improve the quality of education. Becoming involved in 'improvement' is not only about becoming 'better' but also to do with becoming 'different' through questioning the taken-for-grantedness, the habits, the comfort blankets that we wrap around ourselves from time to time and by adopting a more problem-posing teaching posture. Fundamentally this is about having a certain professional disposition (see Principle 5, Chapter 2). It is about questioning practice with confidence so as to open up new possibilities and new directions for action.

Critical reflection that leads to improved action tackles the context, or the 'system' in which teaching is embedded. It does this by asking challenging questions such as:

- Whose interests are served and denied by my/our practice?
- What conditions nourish and constrain my/our practice?
- What organisational and other influences prevent me/us working in alternative ways?
- What alternatives are available to me/us?

Critical reflection is more than just reflecting on practice in a speculative way. Reflecting critically implies a commitment to at least try to improve practice, policy and the 'system' within which practice is embedded and policy is generated. It is a creative process.

The reflective moments in the action research process are given relatively scant attention. It is often caricatured as a private, solitary, introspective activity with the main cognitive process of 'replay and rehearsal' helping the practitioner to make sense of practice. We often hear teachers say, 'We just mull things over'. There is no definitive and correct way of doing action research. The same can be said of reflecting-on-practice. To maximise its potency, however, reflection needs to be both structured and supported and the interests it serves sorted out.

In a recent review of approaches to reflection, Ghaye and Lillyman (1997) identified four interests that reflection might serve. This links us back to Principle 6 in Chapter 2 and reflection being 'interest serving'. They are as follows:

1. *A personal interest:* reflection on personal agendas, emotionality, self-study and enhancing feelings of self-worth and identity.
2. *A learning through experience interest:* reflection on past actions. An active exploration on teachers' own and others' experiences. This requires practitioners to value their own experience and have an openness that enables them to learn from the experiences of others (Kolb 1984).
3. *A competency-based interest:* reflection focused on skill development, problem-solving, and improvements in the technical and practical domains of educational work.
4. *A transformatory interest:* reflection that challenges the *status quo*, challenges the oppressive and disempowering influences on practice and tackles the barriers to improvement.

The reflective moments in the ongoing action research process are so very important. Reflection is like the glue that holds the research process together. It is misleading to think that it is 'fourth-in-line' in the cycle of events and 'done at the end' before formulating a new, improved action plan.

Reflection on action is a complex business. It is wise for action researchers to appreciate that there are a number of conceptualisations of reflection, some of which may be more appropriate and supportive of their intention to improve practice and the context in which it takes place, than others. For example, some conceptualisations of reflection are:

1. *as a dichotomy* of reflection-in-action and reflection-on-action (Schön 1983, 1987). The latter is a retrospective interrogation of practice to come to know the knowledge used and the feelings that accompanied action within a particular situation. The process of *reframing* lies at the heart of this conceptualisation. It is a process where data drawn from our practice is seen differently;
2. *as intentional activity* (Ghaye 1996a) in that we reflect on purpose and with a purpose in mind. It is no accident that we reflect. Something usually triggers it;
3. *as for knowledge and skill development* (Benner 1984, Steinmaker and Bell 1979) where reflection is claimed to develop and enhance particular cognitive, affective, and psychomotor skills;
4. *as creating practitioner-derived knowledge* (Smyth 1991) that is worthy, valid, and relevant to particular educational situations;
5. *as resolving problematic situations* and the basis for problem-based learning (Dewey 1933, Schön 1991, Woods 1994) where systematic reflections enable us to think through and resolve educational situations that we perceive as being characterised by uncertainty, disorder and indeterminacy;
6. *as a process of becoming different* (Giroux 1987) in which reflection helps to equip us with lenses to read the world critically in order to improve it.

Having thought this through the action researcher might then be well advised to clarify which function(s) reflection is to serve. For example, the function of reflection might be:

1. *to act as a bridge* (Silcock 1994) from tacit knowledge to considered action and from the practice world of educational settings to the process of theory generation;
2. *to enhance the quality of action* (Olsen 1992) in that it enables us to talk about our practice (critically reflective conversations with self and others) and to practise different things. Reflection without action is just wishful thinking (Freire 1972);
3. *to increase accountability* (Diamond 1991) because the principles of technocratic efficiency emphasise hierarchically structured, top–down models of accountability with an increasing burden for professional accountability residing with the individual practitioner;
4. *as a much-needed counter discourse* (Smyth 1991) to challenge the ensconced and pervasive technicist views of educational practice that marginalise and delegitimise the teaching experiences, histories and practical wisdom that practitioners use in mediating their lives. This counter discourse is no less important for student teachers. The point Whitty *et al.* (1987) made over a decade ago is still pertinent.

> It is still possible to foster a spirit of critical reflection amongst student teachers. Indeed, their experience on teaching practice of declining material conditions and teacher morale generates a positive demand for critical reflection not only on their own practice but upon the ways in which state policy impinges upon it.
>
> (Whitty *et al.* 1987: 174).

Action research for improving thinking, practice and working context takes as its starting point the socially-constructed, value-laden nature of practice. Action for improvement can be usefully conceived as a dialogical and reflective process. Action research is not only about learning – it is about knowledge production and about a commitment to improve practice. We believe that the principles and practices of action research can play a significant part in helping us all to establish, sustain, and nourish new and more meaningful work environments. If action research cannot promise to be empowering, liberating, and emancipatory, if it cannot promise to develop 'enchanted' workplaces, what is the least that it could claim? We feel that the most humble claim should be that it might give us a greater sense of control over our own work and free us somewhat to increase our avenues for alternative action. Perhaps for these reasons alone we should give action research serious consideration and the part reflection-on-practice plays in this process.

The personal: a development profile

The third important source of influence that can illustrate the links between teaching, evidence and reflection is the 'personal'. Teachers do or do not improve their practice according to whether they perceive a need to address anything in their teaching that is problematic. This might be good practice that needs further nourishment or perceived areas of weakness that need strengthening. Perceiving a need is a first step. Action to improve the situation is dependent upon the teacher feeling able to act. This involves having the emotional strength, professional commitment and intellectual capacity to improve practice within the culture and context of their school. Personal improvement needs to be justified and related to the teacher's values. It can be documented and reflected upon if set out in the form of a profile (Husbands 1993).

What follows is an example of a personal development profile. We briefly put this in context. Since the early 1990s in the UK the Department for Education has promoted profiling and competency-based approaches to professional development (DfE 1992a, 1993a). This movement is part of a 'cradle-to-grave profiling system, going from initial teacher training through induction to further profesional development' (Hutchinson 1994: 303).

A profile is where student teachers are required to gather evidence of their professional development throughout their course and present this evidence to others. Students are encouraged to reflect on key aspects of their teaching and to look for ways to demonstrate that they have acquired certain skills and understood key concepts. Their practice is regularly and thoroughly monitored by a range of assessors such as teachers, mentors, tutors and exterma; examiners, who feed back, advise and comment on their progress. They offer constructive criticism, support networks and ways forward with the intention of helping student teachers to become more effective teachers.

Being told where strengths and weaknesses lie is one thing; being able to identify and articulate these yourself is quite another. Providers of initial teacher training have spent considerable amounts of time and money on deciding 'what makes a good teacher?' Elaborate and detailed profiling documents have been conceived and implemented in order to help students document their needs and set personal targets.

Following the publication of the *Standards for the Award of Qualified Teacher Status* (DfEE 1997), the Faculty of Eduaction and Psychology at University College Worcester revised their profiling system to accommodate the new requirements. The profile aimed to help student teachers reflect on their practice and identify where improvements could be made. With the support of a mentor, tutor and, in some cases, a friend, all students engage in a dialogue, based on the profile, where perceived strengths and weaknesses are openly discussed. Comments are recorded by the student and feedback is offered by the mentor with targets set for those areas that need to be addressed. Students are expected to use the profile regularly and are responsible for the gathering of evidence. The teacher or mentor verifies the student's entries on evidence forms and offers constructive feedback and/or targets. Tables 4.1–4.4 show examples from a third year student teacher's profile. Jolanda has looked for evidence of her progress in the following areas:

- Planning
- Teaching and Class Management
- Assessment, Recording, Reporting, Monitoring and Accountability
- Professional Attitude and Awareness.

These relate directly to the categories identified in the standards for newly qualified teachers (DfEE 1997) and Jolanda records, in the 'focus' column, the particular standards to which she is referring.

Her evidence includes reference to:

- schemes of work
- pupils' work
- tutor observations
- National Curriculum requirements

- short and medium term planning
- evaluations of lessons
- teacher/mentor comments
- pupil relationships

and so on.

Table 4.1 Evidence sheet for B: PLANNING

DATE	FOCUS (Standards)	EVIDENCE (completed by student) *What do I do and what did I learn?*	FEEDBACK/TARGETS (completed by teacher/mentor)
19/05/98	*c*	I evaluate each of my lessons critically and use my assessment of pupils' achievements to make changes and strengthen any weaknesses.	*Looking at your notes, I feel that in some instances you may be over-critical. Remember learning is a two way process. However well you teach, the children need to do their part!*
20/05/98	*e, d*	In my planning I state the National Curriculum programmes of study for the specific subject area as well as any cross-curricular links. I also make a note in the learning outcomes which address pupils' spiritual, moral, personal and social development.	*You have shown yourself to be very aware and sensitive to the needs of individual children. Your planning is clearly linked to the National Curriculum. Think about how you can organise group A to get better cooperation.*
25/05/98	*ai, ii, iii, iv*	I had originally planned to teach just the Year 2 children in today's creative writing lesson due to the usual year group split. However my teacher asked me to take the Year 1 children also, which I did. I managed to rethink the lesson and questioning so that this age group was catered for and so that the task was set with realistic expectations for all children involved.	*Your planning is good and it is pleasing to see that it is also adaptable and able to be differentiated when necessary. You were flexible in your approach today and modified your plans accordingly.*
26/05/98	*aii, iii, c, d*	In the maths practical weighing lesson the Year 2 children had to work in larger groups than I had originally planned for due to lack of resources. This was quite challenging for some of the children who find if difficult to share and work alongside others. However it was a good opportunity to observe them and make a note of what needs to be reinforced when they next do group practical work.	*It is difficult to plan in an ideal way without adequate equipment. Our numbers in school have risen very sharply over the last 18 months which means that equipment resources need enhancing when funds permit. Think about alternative ways to organise a lesson such as this.*

Table 4.2 Evidence Sheet For B: Teaching And Class Management

DATE	FOCUS (Standards)	EVIDENCE (completed by student) *What do I do and what did I learn?*	FEEDBACK/TARGETS (completed by teacher/mentor)
18/05/98	*ki, iv, x, xi, xiv*	I make effective use of the classroom displays in order to enhance and reinforce learning. I have completed another display illustrating the children's work on light. It is a cross-curricular display and shows photos of children at work. I have made it interactive by the use of questions and other written sources. I have made sure that the children are aware of this new display and its purpose.	*Your displays are very impressive. They show the children's work to best advantage and encourage further thinking. Try to bring some of the written work to the children's eye level so that they can all enjoy it and not just the adults!*
19/05/98	*n*	I take a critical and reflective approach as well as actively seeking the advice of my teacher and my own knowledge to evaluate each of my lessons.	*You are able to stand back and be objective about the lesson you have taught. You have taken advice and acted on it.*
20/05/98	*f, g, h, ki, v, vi, viii*	In today's science lesson the children were arranged for work in groups. I sat with each group to make sure all were on-task and using their time productively. I made the rules clear at the start of the lesson, e.g. they needed to share and I stopped them on occasion to reinforce things. I used careful questioning.	*A well-thought-out lesson, planned and thoroughly researched. A confident presentation and excellent questioning technique. When working with one group keep your eye on the others!*
01/06/98	*f, i, j, ki, ii, iii, iv, v, vi, vii, viii, ix, m*	Today I took a whole-class science investigation on electricity. I made sure all the children knew the safety rules. Sometimes it was difficult to keep all the children involved especially with three new children. I managed this by various questioning techniques so that each age group could contribute. I also did whole-class predictions where all children contributed.	*The three new children were those visiting for the day who will be starting full time after summer holidays. A well-managed, but not easy, lesson with the age range involved. You need to be aware of the group sitting in the far corner who could not see your examples on the board very well.*
28/05/98	*f, g, h, ki, xiii*	I am having difficulties keeping some of the Year 2 children, five in particular, on-task during some lessons. I have tried a variety of strategies such as praise, reward, targets, moving them, sitting next to them, supporting them, etc. but I haven't found any of these to be successful at all times so I am still trying to find another strategy that works.	*Keep trying! There are some children who resist for one reason or another whatever you do. It does make you feel better when colleagues further on in the school have the same problems with the same children! Keep flexible and keep trying alternatives.*

Table 4.3 Evidence Sheet for C: Monitoring, Assessment, Recording, Reporting and Accountability

DATE	FOCUS (Standards)	EVIDENCE (completed by student) *What do I do and what did I learn?*	FEEDBACK/TARGETS (completed by teacher/mentor)
13/05/98	*ci*	I try and circulate round each table in the classroom to check, by questioning, the children to see what they have understood and therefore to monitor their knowledge and understanding.	*You can combine this questioning with observation of work being produced and how the children are coping with the practical aspects of the task.*
14/05/98	*a, ciii*	I try to critically evaluate each of my lessons and especially make a note of what needs to be improved for the next lesson and also what the children need to revisit. I then use this information to write my lesson plans.	*I'm all for being thorough. It is important at this stage of learning! Make it clear, on your lesson plans, how you have used assessment information.*
14/05/98	*b*	I set each child their own aims for each lesson, whether it be hand-writing skills, presentation, punctuation, behaviour or whatever the aim of that lesson may be. I try to give constructive feedback to each child.	*That is an ideal to aim for, but in practical terms not always easy to achieve, everytime.*
18/05/98	*a, d, e, i*	I understand the role of monitoring, assessment, recording and reporting, e.g. when planning future lessons, for my own need, parental need, the next class teacher's need and in particular the child's needs so that work can be at his/her own level. I critically reflect on each lesson to see whether or not the children have successfully responded to the tasks and achieved the learning intentions.	*Children and their work produced have been consistently monitored and any extension work planned accordingly. Record-keeping in maths is particularly good. Try and use this system with other subjects too.*
19/05/98	*a, ci, cii, iv*	I assess the children's progress through their outcomes, questioning them and observing them at work. I keep a diagnostic record for a range of children which illustrates their strengths and weaknesses in each subject area and tasks.	*Your diagnostic records have been thorough, with thought given to the strengths and weaknesses of individual pupils.*
19/05/98	*b, civ*	I always mark the children's work. Where possible I do this with them at my side so that I can give oral and written feedback which is constructive and gives them a new aim for that specific piece of work.	*Well done! At this age you need to have children with you while you mark to explain what you have done and where they need to aim in order to improve.*

Table 4.4 Evidence Sheet for D: Professional Attitude and Awareness

DATE	FOCUS (Standards)	EVIDENCE (completed by student) *What do I do and what did I learn?*	FEEDBACK/TARGETS (completed by teacher/mentor)
18/05/98	*g*	I make every effort to contribute to school-based activities. This has been achieved through netball and football matches as well as helping in swimming lessons for the last weeks of my practice. I have also made good and friendly relationships with a large group of parents and other adults in the school.	*You have taken an active interest in all aspects of school life and occasions while you have been here.*
18/05/98	*c, d, e*	I always set good and positive examples to the children I teach and am very eager to further my personal and professional development.	*You are always eager to improve and progress. You do realise that this is an ongoing process for the next 30 or so years?!*
24/05/98	*e*	I asked my teacher to take my teaching file home with her so that she could look at my lesson plans and make sure I was covering all aspects. Fortunately she had no criticism for me but I am always ready to accept any criticism as this helps to inform my planning and management for future lessons.	*A very comprehensive file. You have put a lot of time into this and emerged with a useful working document. Continue as you are and remain determined to improve your knowledge and technique.*
02/06/98	*f, h*	I discussed the behaviour policy with the headteacher today and also the role of governors in the school. I will be meeting the chair of governors at tomorrow's open day.	*After an incident in the playground you checked the school's behaviour policy and acted accordingly. Your meeting with governors tomorrow will be interesting.*

Each section in the profile also includes a summary description or 'portrait' of the kinds of qualities, knowledge and skills that may be expected of student teachers. These portraits range from descriptions of students who are not successfully meeting the standards to those who are highly proficient and progressing well. They highlight key aspects of the teacher's role and they also serve as a summary of the overall achievements of the student teacher. Each 'stage description' is intended to help students, teachers and mentors have a meaningful discussion about the type of teacher that the student would like to be and the type of teacher that they actually are. Below are the stage descriptions used to assess Jolanda's 'Planning' in the third year.

The agreed stage description is documented in the profile as a summative assessment of the student's school experience. The students take their profiles with them from semester to semester and year to year, supplementing the profile with information as they move through their course. This highlights the range of experiences that the students encounter and the impact of these experiences on their personal and professional development.

Stage 1

The student is operating at a *SUPPORTED* level in terms of planning within the given context. Lesson plans are *sketchy* and require a *significant input* by the class teacher/mentor in order to reach a satisfactory standard. There is *little understanding* of learning intentions or outcomes and *no* evidence to suggest that the student can articulate these when asked about the purpose of a lesson. Individual needs are *rarely* considered and plans accommodate *one* level of ability only. The student *relies on* teacher/mentor guidance for planning *group work* and addressing *individual* pupils' needs. Plans are *rarely* related to the National Curriculum programmes of study and to the school's long and medium term plans. The student *experiences difficulties* when attempting to explain *how* lessons will be taught and relating this to the written plans. Tasks set for individuals and groups *occasionally* maintain the pupils' interest but *only* when support is provided by the teacher/mentor. *Some* pupils meet the desired learning outcomes as stated in the student's lesson plan but the student *finds it difficult* to *recognise* when weaknesses in planning have affected the outcomes of a lesson. The student shows *little awareness* of the need to *support* children with special educational needs and the need to *consider* pupils' spiritual, moral, personal, social and cultural development. The role of assessment and the need to build this into future planning is *omitted* from the planning process.

Stage 2

The student demonstrates a *SATISFACTORY* understanding of the role of planning within the given context. Lesson plans cover the necessary requirements with lessons well thought out and prepared and learning objectives *clearly* stated. *Differentiation* is *carefully* considered when planning for individuals, groups and *whole class* activities. Plans are *based on* the National Curriculum programmes of study and *complement* the school's long and medium term plans. The student *shows an interest* in discussing *how* lessons will be taught and relates this to the written plans. Tasks set for the pupils *generally* maintain *high* levels of interest with the *majority* of children meeting the desired outcomes. The student is able to *reflect* on lessons and to *identify* where weaknesses in planning have affected the outcomes of a lesson and *suggest* ways to make improvements. The student is *making progress* in *supporting* children with special educational needs and in *promoting* pupils' spiritual, moral, personal, social and cultural development. The role of assessment and the need to build this into future planning is being addressed *primarily* in *core* subject work.

Stage 3

The student demonstrates a *COMPETENT* understanding of the role of planning within the given context. Lesson plans are *thorough and well presented* with each lesson *carefully considered* and prepared. Learning objectives are *clearly* stated and presented. *Differentiation* is *an integral part* of the planning for both individual, group and *whole class* activities. Plans are *directly* related to the National Curriculum programmes of study and to the school's long and medium term plans. The student *actively* seeks to discuss *how* lessons will be taught and relates this to written plans. Tasks set for groups and the *whole class* maintain *good* levels of interest with the *majority* of children meeting the desired outcomes. The student is seen to be *reflective* and able to identify where improvements can be made. The student is *keen* to *plan for* children with special educational needs and to *promote* pupils' spiritual, moral, personal, social and cultural development. The role of assessment and the need to build this into future planning is *evident* in the *core* subjects and in *some foundation* subjects.

Stage 4

The student demonstrates a *HIGHLY PROFICIENT* understanding of the role of planning within the given context. Lesson plans are *coherent and thoughtful* with a range of *realistic expectations* for all pupils. Learning intentions and outcomes are *clearly* stated and presented. Work is *carefully differentiated* to accommodate all abilities in group and *whole class* activities. National Curriculum programmes of study are *integral* to planning and suitably matched to the school's long and medium term plans with some relevant individual interpretation included. The student *actively* seeks to discuss *how* lessons will be taught and relates this to written plans. Tasks set for groups and the whole class maintain *high* levels of interest with *all* pupils meeting the desired outcomes. The student is *critically reflective* and indicates where plans can be strengthened to ensure *progression*. The student is able to *identify and address* special educational needs and to *promote* pupils' spiritual, moral, personal, social and cultural development. The role of assessment and the need to build this into future planning is *well developed* in the core subjects and is *carefully considered* in the foundation subjects.

Profiles are seen as 'working documents' which are reflected on both at the time of writing, in relation to the student's current school context, and also in subsequent years, when an overview of the student's experience in a variety of school settings forms the basis of a reflective conversation with a personal tutor. Following the publication of the Career Entry Profile (TTA 1997b) student teachers, on completion of their course, use the College profile as a form of evidence to identify strengths and priorities for further professional development. Targets for their first year of teaching are then identified by the student teacher and the profile is taken with them into their first post. An action plan is jointly agreed between the student teacher and a nominated mentor in school and used as the basis for further professional development in the newly qualified teacher's induction year.

Using profiles, both in a formative and summative way, should not be regarded as unproblematic. There is normally an expectation by providers of initial teacher training that student teachers will manage the profiling process themselves and be responsible for the gathering of evidence regarding their professional development. This takes a certain degree of skill, motivation and confidence, and an ability to recognise where professional development has indeed taken place. Only with the support of mentors, teachers, tutors and peers, can most students reflect on their emerging professionality and identify where there is evidence to show that they are learning and evolving as student teachers. This brings with it questions relating to how manageable a profiling system is, how valid the student's evidence is and who has owner-ship of the profile. Without the involvement of other professionals and without sustained, reflective conversations on the profile, it becomes yet another course requirement which may be perceived by the student as time-consuming, pointless and insignificant. To make profiling worthwhile, student teachers need to know that they will receive feedback, constuctive criticism and support. The profile facilitates reflection-on-practice. It is a process of creating a 'text' about the work of the teacher. Creating a text is one thing; interpreting it and then using it to move thinking and practice forward is something else. We address these issues in the following chapter.

CHAPTER FIVE

Reflection-on-improvement: The Validation Of Practice

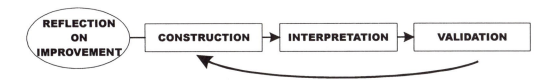

Student teachers are often asked on school experience, 'How might the lesson have been improved?' This can be received in a number of ways. Sometimes it is decoded and felt to imply that the lesson was not very good, things went wrong, the supervising tutor and class teacher are unhappy. It is interpreted to mean, 'Please do not do it like that again' and 'Let's think seriously about changing things'. Another interpretation is that the lesson was far from being a 'disaster' and that the tutor and/or class teacher are trying to help pinpoint certain aspects of the lesson which might be further strengthened. There is another view too, which is that this is the kind of question that conscientious and reflective teachers ask themselves all the time. When the word 'improvement' is used it brings with it a range of thoughts and emotions. Some are rather more negative and relate to teacher deficits. Others are embedded in conceptions of what it means to be a professional, of teacher development as a lifelong learning process and associated with nourishing strengths as well as working at relatively weaker areas of practice.

If, as we have argued, the fundamental purpose of reflective practice is to improve the quality of education, then we must ask the question, 'So, what does improvement mean?' Improvements in individual and collective workplace competence are inextricably linked to changes in the quality of human interactions. Just as we need to question the notion and processes of change, so too do we need to question the slippery concept of improvement. Not all change may be considered to be improvement. Similarly, what is thought to be an improvement for a particular work environment, say in one particular class, is not inevitably and always seen to be supportive of the interests of all those who work in other classrooms.

Ghaye (1995) argues that workplace improvement needs to be considered in relation to five questions. Each question needs to be reflected on and talked about in school.

1. *The question of time*
   - When are the most appropriate times for our improvement efforts to take place?
   - When are the consequences of these improvements likely to be felt and noticed?
2. *The question of scale*
   - What is the scope of the improvement?
   - How many people are involved, and what resources will it consume?
   - What is the nature, magnitude, and educative potency of the consequences of the envisioned improvement?
3. *The question of uncertainty*
   - For example, how far can we be sure that the new conditions, action, motivations and orientations are indeed an improvement?
   - What does valid evidence of improvement look like?
   - How far do we understand the links between perceived improvements and concrete and visible improvements in the quality of educational interactions in the workplace?
   - Are these improvements real or imagined?
4. *The question of micropolitics*
   Institutional politics provoke questions that are central to any improvement effort. Improvement is a value-laden concept and process. It is therefore not surprising that people in a particular work environment think differently and want to act differently in order to influence and shape their future and the futures of others. Understanding the politics of teacher improvement efforts is a recognition that, in school, there is inevitably an interplay between competing interests. Reflective practice will raise political questions because improvement is concerned with 'interests', 'power', and the resolution of 'conflict'. Improvement can be seen as who gets what, where, how, when and why?
5. *The question of penetration*
   Sometimes, because of weak or misguided improvement efforts and external pressures, we pay too much attention to the impressionistic and the facade that decorates the surface of our work environments. This is at the expense of working at those things that are more fundamental and that give rise and tend to sustain these 'surface' attributes. Perhaps teachers have grown accustomed to improving things without paying sufficient attention to the culture of schools on which their improvement efforts are predicated. School improvement is one thing. However school transformation is different because it penetrates deeply and improves the quality of the educational relationships of all those in the organisation. This deep kind of penetration involves the careful management of both the external and internal school structures and influences. Too much emphasis on internal development will not lead to school transformation. The connection with the wider environment is vital for this (Fullan 1994).

Improvement cannot take place unless we learn from experience. Failure to do this is resigning ourselves to being prisoners of our past. Reflection-on-practice is intentional action; the intention is to improve education through a rigorous reflection of the learning that has accrued as a consequence of engaging in the practitioner-research process which we outlined in Chapter 4. In a reflective account the learning from experience needs to be transparent. The reader should be able to *see* the professional landscape in which the writer is working. The reader should *hear* the way the reflective dialogues have moved thinking and practice forward. The writer should also attend to the way his or her account helps the reader to *feel* and empathise with the teacher's workplace achievements and ongoing struggles.

Reflections on learning from experience are predicated on three things. First, that experience must be had, it cannot be taught (Munby and Russell 1995: 173). Secondly, that we can make some sense of what is happening around us. Thirdly, that we are able to communicate this in some understandable manner. We can call a product of reflection a 'text' or 'account'. Making sense of teaching is always a learning process. Reflection helps us to become more aware of the potency of our experience and what we can take from it to move our thinking and practice forward. Miller and Boud (1996) offer some important views in relation to this. They are that:

- experience is the foundation of, and stimulus for, learning;
- learners actively construct their own experience;
- learning is holistic;
- learning is socially and culturally constructed;
- learning is influenced by the socio-emotional context in which it occurs.

(pp. 9–10)

Central to this chapter are Miller and Boud's ideas that what teachers (and children) experience is influenced by their own unique past, the current learning milieu and future expectations. Secondly, that while teachers and children construct their own learning, they do so in the context of a particular social setting, namely that of the school with its own values and things that it regards as worthwhile. Thirdly, that learning from experience is a social, cognitive and affective activity. We have argued earlier (see Chapter 1) that reflection-on-practice has an important emotional component.

> Emotions and feelings are key pointers both to possibilities for, and barriers to, learning. Denial of feelings is a denial of learning. It is through emotions that some of the tensions and contradictions between our own interests and those of the external context manifest themselves.
>
> (Miller and Boud 1996: 10)

Creating a text: the reflective learning journal

Journal writing is an important aid to making sense of teaching and learning (Ghaye and Lillyman 1997). We discuss it in some detail here. Journals form a part of many initial teacher training and continuing professional development courses. They are a popular aid to reflection and they are also about the construction and interpretation of meaning. What follows are our responses to the questions that we are most frequently asked when introducing the idea of reflective journals.

What is a learning journal?

This can be answered by looking at its contents and how they are communicated. A learning journal should contain the teacher's practical knowledge and wisdom. *What* is written about is the content. When written down, a 'text' is created which enables teachers to re-examine fundamental issues associated with teaching and learning and the contexts which mould it. The text can comprise a range of evidence and be written in a creative and interpretative manner so that the meanings, which reveal themselves from the re-examination of journal entries at a later date, can inform future practice. Choosing what to write about is often difficult, for everything seems relevant at times. The bottom line is that the content can be justified as being professionally significant, at that moment in time. Learning journals serve many purposes which in turn influence what teachers write in them. For example, they can be a repository for evidence about children's learning, for examining changes in your self-image, as an evaluation mechanism for aspects of your practice, to facilitate critical thinking, to release feelings and frustrations and to see different 'truths'.

How the phenomenon is written about, the mediums and genres used, is the writing process. Learning accrues from this process and is facilitated by responses to questions such as, 'What kind of teacher am I?', 'How have I come to teach this way?' and 'How can I improve my practice?' Teachers know their practical worlds in general, social and shared ways and also in unique and personal ways. In constructing accounts of practice the past is not irrelevant but provides a context for present thinking, action and future intentions.

When do I write my learning journal?

Entries should be made regularly; we suggest at least once each week. Learning has to be given a chance to emerge so teachers need to make a series of entries and then re-read them to search for patterns, themes, issues, conflicts and so on. It is often useful to keep a small notebook to jot down the essence of interesting, satisfying, worrying and/or puzzling encounters and conversations as you go through the week. These can then be elaborated upon in the learning journal later. The longer the writing is left, the more you have to trust your memory!

What interests do learning journals serve?

We have drawn upon the work of Thomas (1992, 1995) to develop a number of 'portraits' to illuminate the interests learning journals might serve.

Portrait 1:   The learning journal as 'A collection of anecdotes'
Personal anecdotes are experiences and so have a value. A collection of anecdotal evidence may reveal something worthwhile about a teacher's thinking, feelings and practice. To be more useful the anecdotes need to be placed in a context and need to be re-visited, re-read and evaluated over time. If anecdotes tell you nothing about how to improve what you do, then you need to change the content and process.

Portrait 2:   The learning journal as 'An interpreted story'
Just as stories have structures, entries in a journal can also be structured. An entry might usefully have a clear beginning and a middle. It might not have an end, just a range of 'messy-bits' and unresolved issues. As with story making the content needs to be carefully selected and certain aspects of the entry given more emphasis than others. Journal entries of this kind, just like stories, have to be interpreted. Out of this comes the learning.

Portrait 3:   The learning journal as 'A fulcrum for professional development'
Some of the characteristics of learning-enriched work environments are collegiality, open communication, trust, support and help. Having the time to talk through the problems of practice is also a vital ingredient of both personal and collective professional development. For some the learning journal fulfils a need to tell, to enter into dialogues and to expose and explore various interpretations of 'This is what I did, for these reasons. This is what it felt like, so what do you think?'

Portrait 4:   The learning journal as 'A means of asserting that teaching is evidence-based'
This can be done if entries are guided by the following ideas:

- you are trying to live out the things you believe in;
- you wish to account for your actions;
- you are actively seeking to improve your practice;
- you acknowledge that claims for moving practice forward have to be supported with evidence.

Portrait 5:   The learning journal as 'A means of bringing order to turbulent educational environments'
In trying to make sense of our educational worlds we need to hold the turbulence still for a moment. A single journal entry is a piece of frozen text waiting to be reflected upon. For a moment it brings a kind of order to things. Teachers are not confronted with issues, challenges, dilemmas and problems that are independent of each other, but with dynamic, turbulent and often chaotic situations which interact simultaneously. Ackoff (1979) calls such situations 'messes'. Journal writing has the potential to help us make sense of such 'messes'.

Portrait 6:   The learning journal as 'A means of searching for the truth'
Each journal entry should not be viewed as some absolute, fixed and verifiable truth i.e. the last and final word on the matter under consideration. Teaching is value-laden so truths are often partial, contested, intersubjective and elusive. Learning through reflection on journal entries is a continuous process of redefinition and reconstruction. It is a creative enterprise.

Portrait 7:   The learning journal as 'A basis for building a better world'
Journals should have a prospective quality. Constructive and critical reflections on past events should constitute a new beginning or an action plan to improve what is already being experienced and in existence.

What are the ethical implications of keeping a learning journal?

Moving thinking and practice forward requires not only expertise and commitment but also honesty and integrity. We have grouped some of the more obvious ethical issues associated with journal writing under three headings. These are rights, risks and benefits, and consent.

The issue of rights
When teachers reflect on their practice through their journal they have certain rights. These are

related to self-respect, self-esteem and dignity. Whether or not teachers keep their journal entries to themselves or share them in some way, they have the right to self-determination. No teacher should be coerced into making public what is written in their journal: they have the right to privacy. The owner of the journal should be the one who determines the time, extent and context under which they disclose their journal entries. Teachers have the right to decide what to withhold and what they share. If teachers share the contents of their journal with others it is important that this issue of rights is sorted out early on.

The issue of risks and benefits
In keeping a learning journal feelings of discomfort and vulnerability may arise because teachers are asking questions such as, 'Why is my teaching like this?', 'How did it come to be this way?' and 'How can I improve it?' A commitment to learn from journal writing is a commitment to a great deal of introspection, honesty with self and a frame of mind that will be able to handle what you come to know in a constructive way. Sharing your journal entries with others may also put at risk such things as your level of self-confidence, call into question aspects of your practice and challenge your much cherished professional values. There are also risks for those who support or facilitate reflection through journal writing such as teacher educators and school mentors. What should or must they do for example if they hear an account of malpractice or teaching which they would consider as unprofessional? What happens to notions of trust and confidentiality between people in such circumstances? Who becomes vulnerable, perhaps marginalised or peripheralised? Questions such as 'How far is the account true?', 'How far are we sure of it?' and 'What are the risks associated with not being sure?' need to be asked and responded to.

The issue of consent
It is important to think through this issue if, in the contents of the journal, teachers are drawing upon the experiences of colleagues as a means to further their own ends. If journal entries are made public and shared, for example, with peers, issues about who is telling what, to whom and why, need to be clarified. Additionally the general dialogical environment needs to be supportive of this activity and requires some warmth and collective engagement. In listening to another's account we are given an entrée into someone else's educational world. In disclosing what is in a learning journal, the 'teller' needs to be sure that they can trust others with what may be a sensitive but certainly a professionally significant issue.

What are some of the tensions that need to be resolved in keeping a learning journal?

The contents and processes of keeping a journal are held in a 'tensioned' relationship. Some of the most important tensions that need resolving are discussed.

Tension 1:   Between writing personal and safe responses
Developing teacher professionality through journal writing requires the development of an ability to write what you feel needs writing in a fair, accurate and honest manner and often to say things in a critical yet constructive way. Sometimes safe responses are written in a context of fear, disempowerment and blame. Sometimes they are written up so as not to offend if they were to enter the public domain in some way.

Tension 2:   Between teacher-centric and 'significant other' perspectives
The journal is a medium through which the teacher can present their view of things (see types of reflection in Chapter 2). No account is free from bias and a certain amount of distortion (wilful or unconscious); no account is neutral and impartial. The journal can be used to represent alternative perspectives that allow the teacher to see the same teaching incident in different ways. It can serve to illuminate the subjective connections of self with significant others (e.g. teacher colleagues, parents, governors).

Tension 3:   Between privacy and the right to know
This is a complex and very 'contested' issue. We have said that teachers have the right to keep the contents of a learning journal private if they so wish. But this raises the moral problem concerning the rights others have to know the content of the journal. Some of these rights are to do with journal writing in a context of professional and organisational accountability. Other rights are more legalistic in kind and relate to the way evidence from a journal might be used in a process of litigation. Then there is the right that some might exercise in terms of 'I have the right to know what it is you are writing about me!' This is about the right to know and the right to intervene in the light of that information. Rights are problematic because they often contain appeals to different political, professional and moral values (Pring 1988).

Tension 4:   Between structure and freedom
Sometimes, if keeping a learning journal is an initial teacher training or in-service course requirement, expectations are raised about how far there is a predetermined structure or format for each entry. Keeping a learning journal offers teachers the freedom to express themselves in whatever style they choose, unfettered by 'academic' conventions and traditions.

Tension 5:   Between the particular and the general
One journal entry is an account of a particular instance of practice, an encounter, a dialogue, a feeling, an achievement and so on. It is dangerous to read too much into one entry. Journals that contain numerous entries over time provide the potential for generalisation. This might be a generalisation about a personally-preferred value position in relation to effective learning, about a general strategy for managing a full and busy classroom and so on. In this sense 'general' means what a teacher tends to generally do, think and feel. It may or may not be generally true for others. It is important to appreciate the difference between what is generally the case for one teacher and what is not. In reflecting on journal entries it is also important to try to tease out what is particular and different in certain teaching situations and what are the more patterned, regular and therefore, more general, things. If teachers make these general things known to others, they give them the opportunity to generalise from it to their own teaching situation. This is called naturalistic generalisation (Stake 1995).

Tension 6:   Between moving forward and disillusionment
The learning that accrues from reflective 'text' construction has to be known and valued by the teacher who is keeping the journal. The benefits have to be articulated in such a way that the teacher feels they are moving forward. This sense of moving forward will often be defined in very personal ways. Without this sense, journal-keeping can quickly lead to disillusionment and to feelings that the process was a 'waste of time'.

What are some of the common problems in keeping a learning journal?

Four of the most common are:

1. *The problem of procrastination:* Particularly if it is felt that keeping a learning journal is unworthy of the attention that initial teacher training or in-service course work assignments/exams appear to warrant.
2. *The problem of superficial and unreflective entries:* There is no virtue in trying to describe and faithfully regurgitate what has happened. The idea is to set out the teaching incident and then to interrogate it through the processes of writing, critical reflection and (in some cases) peer or collegial discussion.
3. *The problem of waning enthusiasm:* To make learning happen it needs to have a chance to take hold and be apprehended. It may help to view the learning journals as a companion, to be committed to make regular entries and re-read them over time.
4. *Unwillingness or inability to reflect:* Reflection-on-practice is not just a cognitive activity but a moral, affective and ethical art form. Teachers need to be encouraged to read about keeping a learning journal, about reflection being a complex activity and about the benefits that arise from structured and supported reflection-on-practice.

Examples of journal writing

There are many ways to create a reflective 'text'. Above all other things each entry must be concerned with something professionally significant and written in the journal in such a way that it makes sense to the teacher who writes it.

There is no real virtue in trying to follow some notions of 'academic convention' each time teachers write in their journal. Teachers need to create the kind of 'text' that we described earlier. A 'text' is something that you can learn from; there are no 'writing rules'. Teachers might usefully let go of any notions that they have of trying to 'get it right first time'. The personal relevance and meaning of the entries are important qualities. In keeping a journal teachers should not get bogged down with issues of 'better' or 'worse', about writing better, tighter, more economically. More important is trying to create entries which allow teachers to search for new angles on professional concerns, biases, fragmented and woolly thinking, new juxtapositions and important associations that perhaps had remained unknown and uncelebrated. It is also important to avoid the 'paralysis by analysis syndrome'. Teachers need to be patient and realistic with what they want to get out of their journal writing. It is unrealistic to think that new, wonderful insights about teaching and learning will emerge, as if by magic, from one or two short entries!

In this chapter we illustrate six of the more common types of journal entry. Each type represents a different way of representing what the teacher wanted to record in their journal. Sometimes a series of entries in a journal might be in the same form. But there is no reason why teachers should not change the form of their entry in the same way that they might change the focus of it. One entry might also embrace more than one form. We have labelled the types of journal entry thus:

- faithful regurgitation,
- off-load,
- extend and revise,

- concept-mapping,
- knotty and messy,
- living contradiction.

There is a natural blurring of the edges between types. In reality each 'text' is often part of a 'tangle-of-texts' (Sumara and Luce-Kapler 1993) which convey a sense of the complexities of teaching and learning. In all of them the writer is clearly positioned within the text.

Example 1: The faithful regurgitation type
The emphasis in entries of this kind is upon 'what I've done'. They tend to be mainly descriptive reflections-on-practice and can be written up in a vivid manner. They are personal views on things.

> *I prepared everything so carefully today, or so I thought. We were due to have our PE lesson, practising our catching and throwing skills and we were going to develop this into a game towards the end of the lesson, introducing large bats. I'd arranged the groups so that each group had at least two children who could hit the ball and one who could catch relatively easily. The children were excited and I had spent 10 minutes in the classroom organising the children and explaining what they were going to do. Each group had a team leader and each person in the group had a job to do and a piece of equipment to collect from the PE store. They had all remembered to bring their kit and were bubbling with excitement. I sent Katy to fetch the key to the PE store. She came back with the message that Mr Johns had the key. So she went to his classroom to be told that Mrs Dickens had the key, or at least she did have it first thing in the morning! And so it went on. Each time Katy returned the children groaned.*
>
> *In the end I decided that we may as well go out onto the field and warm up. For ten minutes we jogged and chased and skipped and jumped, until a triumphant Katy appeared waving the elusive key on the end of a string! The children cheered. We all trooped to the PE store and took out the equipment. Five minutes later it was all set up. Children threw their first ball. A crack of lightning streaked across the sky. Screams went up from all sides. Thunder followed. More screams. We raced to pick up equipment and charged to the hall. Rows of faces greeted us. A parents' meeting, which I had completely forgotten about, had just started and an embarrassed head teacher gave me one of her looks! I turned quickly, motioned to the children to retreat and fumbled my way back to the classroom with 29 deflated children in tow. A complete disaster.*
>
> (Class teacher, Year 2)

Example 2: The off-load type
Entries of this kind tend to be high on emotionality with the teacher often claiming that the entry is 'personal and pertinent'. They contain 'perceptive reflections-on-practice'. They often focus upon an encounter with significant others, often colleagues, and can contain disagreements over educational practice and/or policy. The entry is 'significant' in that it makes us cross, it will not go away, has not resolved itself or has questioned our professionality. Some entries of this type can be quite judgemental. The writing process can be cathartic. Through it we can purge ourselves of pent up emotions (Holly 1989).

If I have another lesson like today, I think I'll pack the job in altogether! I'm persevering with the group story because I want the children to learn that they have to listen to each other and to write collaboratively. There are too many individuals in this class who think that they know best and everyone else should be doing as they say! It makes me so angry when I spend hours encouraging them to be thoughtful and to respect each other and then they just argue and fight and get on each other's nerves. It makes me feel a failure. I can't see why they have to behave in this way when I try to make the lessons enjoyable and different.

(Student teacher, Year 5 class)

Example 3: The extend and revise type

This type can only be found in journals where the teacher has made a number of previous entries. It comes into being through revisiting, reviewing and re-appreciating earlier entries. It is evidence of a systematic and committed approach to reflection-on-practice. With entries of this kind there is an opportunity to do a number of things such as:

- celebrate the good and rewarding aspects of practice;
- re-relieve you of any feelings of frustration;
- remind you of the things that you had forgotten about the incident;
- re-appraise earlier responses to significant incidents;
- look again for values, prejudices and blindspots that get in the way of moving practice forward;
- separate out those things that you have some control over and can influence, from those that you presently cannot control;
- take stock of 'where you are at';
- clarify action plans.

In adopting this style it is important to date each entry. In this way you will be able to place altered or confirmed thoughts, feelings and actions on a time line. This temporal dimension to your journal entries might give you a way into understanding, more richly, notions of professional 'development'.

16th September
I think I am going to find it extremely difficult to work with the other Year 3 teacher, Mrs Jenkins. She has a completely different way of handling the children and managing her classroom and she expects me, as the new teacher, to follow her example. We've almost had two confrontations so far but, each time, I have bitten my tongue because she clearly thinks that she knows best. Perhaps I am not as tolerant as I thought I was but the thought of having to work in the classroom next to her for a whole year is depressing me. I can hear her shout at the children and humiliate them when they have done something wrong and she obviously feels that this is the best way to sort out difficult behaviour. I wonder if she realises what she sounds like.

21st October
Four weeks since I wrote about my arrival as a new teacher to the school. It feels like

four years! I am pleased that I have formed a really good relationship with Mrs Jenkins, despite the fact that we are still poles apart in the way we respond to children's behaviour. On reflection I now know that she is actually very insecure and her attitude is defensive because she cannot find another way to deal with difficult situations other than by shouting. She has even commented on the way I have calmed down some of the 'difficult' children in my class and how she thought I wouldn't stand a chance with my 'softly, softly', approach. A back-handed compliment, I think! I'm trying to teach by example and prove that there are other ways but it's hard to imagine that I can make that much of an impact on such an experienced teacher.

(Newly Qualified Teacher, Year 4)

Example 4: The concept mapping type
Entries of this type are more pictorial or 'graphical' than literary (see Figure 5.2).

Fig. 5.2.

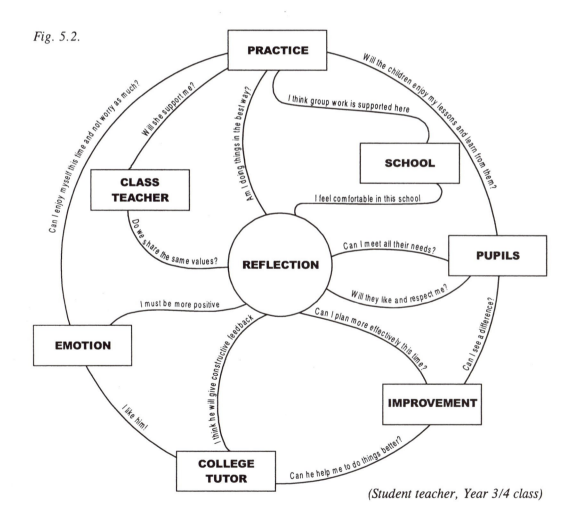

(Student teacher, Year 3/4 class)

A concept map contains teacher knowledge which is represented in the form of a labelled-line graph structure in which the three fundamental elements are nodes, links and relations. We can define the fundamental elements thus:

- *Nodes:* key ideas or concepts
- *Links:* lines drawn between the nodes
- *Relations:* the meaning given to the nodes by the nature of the links between them. In essence concept maps, like journal entries, are personal reality maps, constructed by the teacher. They express the sense or meaning teachers currently have of a particular facet of their work. They are their subjective construction of an aspect of their world. If a journal contains a number of maps which focus on the same area or issue, significant learning can arise because reflection on them can reveal how;
  (a) teachers might fine-tune their 'know that', 'know how' and 'know why' knowledge.
  (b) far ideas remain isolated or more integrated and structured in their mind.
  (c) teachers may have changed their views of aspects of their practice over time.

Example 5: The knotty and messy type

'Knots' have been described by Wagner (1987) as the interrelationship between cognitive and affective processes which lead to conflict and professional dilemmas. Drawing upon theories in cognitive and clinical psychology and psychotherapy, she identifies six types of conflicts or 'knots', some of which might be short lived, others lasting for years. What each type of 'knot' has in common is that they arise due to a discrepancy or dilemma between 'what is' and 'what must or should be'. Knots can affect the quality of teaching. Sometimes we react to knots by complaining. Untying the knots is a learning process. Messy texts (Denzin 1997), as we might describe these entries, are always unfinished, open-ended and can move back and forth from description and interpretation.

> *I was so pleased when I got this promotion to deputy head. I fought off some real competition from other candidates and I know I'm right for the post. But I'm already sensing conflict between still being 'one of the crowd' and working alongside my colleagues and helping them, while also being expected to support the policies of the headteacher and governors, even speaking on their behalf when I'm not sure that I agree with them. It's very difficult to please everyone, especially when I have to say 'no' to invites from staff because I'm working on a policy that needed completing by yesterday! Also I'm not sure that I like being privy to information that staff confided in me before I got this post. Like Mr Sladen saying that he has no respect for the head and can't wait to get out of the school. He's only keeping in the head's good books to make sure that he gets a decent reference for the job that he wants in January! It's a strange feeling to be pulled in so many different directions and I'm not sure how I will cope with it.*
>
> (Deputy head and class teacher, Reception/Year 1)

Example 6: The living contradiction type

We have explained the notion of 'living contradiction' in Chapter 3. Entries focus upon how far teachers are able to live out their values in their practice.

> *When I'm standing in front of my student teachers and we are talking about classroom practice, I can hear myself saying the same things, 'Be positive with the children, find things which they are good at, take the time to listen to them and talk to them about what they enjoy'. The students busily take notes, write up their lesson plans and deliver some interesting and stimulating lessons.*
>
> *And what of my role? Having imparted my words of wisdom and feeling really good about the impact of my teaching on the students, I visit them in schools, observe lessons and give feedback. We talk, I write copious notes for them to look through and I leave the school ready to visit the next student teacher. I pride myself on being a good tutor. When, therefore, I overhear a coment from one of my students saying, 'I wish she wouldn't focus on what I do "wrong" rather than what I do right', it sets me back with a jolt. It suddenly dawns on me that I am doing the complete opposite of what I tell my students to do. I probably do comment on the more negative aspects of their teaching. I'm not sure that I give that much positive feedback or really look for the things that they do particularly well. I think I do spend more time talking than listening to what my students have to say at the end of the lesson and I think, if asked, that I would justify my lack of listening to the fact that I always feel in a rush to get to another school or to get back to College in time to teach.*
>
> *Being confronted with such a contradiction in my own practice has concerned me and made me realise that I need to be very careful about the way I relate to students in future.*
>
> (Higher Education Lecturer/Supervising Tutor)

These examples of 'texts' emphasise the importance of reflecting on particularity and the minutiae of everyday teaching and learning in the search for new knowledge, understandings and sensitivities that serve to improve practice. In turning to chaos theory we find ample support for this belief.

> The modern study of chaos began with the creeping realisation in the 1960s that quite simple mathematical equations could model systems every bit as violent as a waterfall. Tiny differences in input could quickly become overwhelming differences in output ... In weather, for example, this translates into what is only half jokingly known as a butterfly effect – the notion that a butterfly stirring the air today in Peking can transform storm systems next month in New York.
>
> (Gleick 1988: 8)

Reflection on the entries in our learning journals is an attempt to make sense of particular aspects of practice. In the stirrings of these butterfly wings we have the starting point for transforming our understanding about the nature of our professionalism and for improving the quality of education.

The construction of meaning

In making sense of practice through journal writing, we are essentially talking about reality construction and interpretation. This process allows teachers to see and understand particular lessons, objects, utterances or situations in distinctive ways. We are always trying to make sense of our professional lives and using language is how we do it (Harre and Gillett 1994: 127). Reflective practitioners are meaning-makers who appreciate that:

> ... problems do not exist 'out there', ready made, well defined and waiting to be solved. Instead, a problem is seen as a human construct which arises out of a particular perception or interpretation formed about a unique educational context with its values and ends; the values, interests and actions of its inhabitants; and crucially, the particular relation of these features to a theoretical perspective which describes and explains them and their interrelations.
>
> (Parker 1997, 40)

A helpful theoretical perspective is social constructionism (Richardson 1997). This acknowledges that reality is socially constructed and that writing texts is a way of 'framing' reality. It asserts that our way of seeing and interpreting the world is influenced by something other than 'the way the world really is', but 'by our emotions, intentions and purposes – our attitude to existence' (Young 1992: 29). Making sense of teaching and learning is construed as a building or construction process by teachers (and children) interacting with the physical and social world. The challenge it creates for teachers is the problem of multiple perspectives (remember Charlotte's experiences at the start of Chapter 1?). Simply put, we do not all see the world in the same way; reality is not fixed or given. Teachers (and children) partake in its creation (Ravn 1991: 97).

Burr (1995) lists 'the things you would absolutely have to believe, in order to be a social constructionist'. They are:

- a critical stance towards taken-for-granted knowledge.
- historical and cultural specificity (understanding depends upon where and when in the world one lives).
- that knowledge is sustained by social processes (people construct and negotiate understandings of the world between them).
- that knowledge and social action go together (that there are numerous possible constructions of the world. Each construction brings with it or invites a different kind of action).

Classroom realities : Richard's reflections on his practice

Richard is a fourth year primary student teacher who is keeping a reflective learning journal during his final school experience. He has completed a scheme of work on farming in the local environment and carried out a comparative study of farming in a Kenyan village as part of his National Curriculum geography work with his Year 5 children (9–10 years old). He has been particularly concerned with offering the children appropriately differentiated tasks. He talks a lot to them during and after his lessons, monitoring their progress and giving feedback. He reflects on these conversations, which then become the content for his journal. By extending and revising his journal entries, a number of insights have emerged. The knowledge he has personally constructed has a profound effect on his teaching. He comes to understand that his children 'typify' his lessons in certain ways. The most commonly occuring typifications were the extent to which the children perceived his lessons as 'hard/easy', as a desire or otherwise for the lesson to continue and the way the present lesson was or was not perceived as a continuation of the previous lessons.

With regard to the hard/easy typfication Richard writes:

> *It seems that most of the children talk about the lesson as being hard or easy, or in-between. I've been concentrating on trying to present tasks well-matched to the abilities of each child so I've been interested in their comments. One thing I've really learnt is that an apparently straightforward phrase used by Helen such as, 'I thought the lesson was quite easy' meant one thing to her and could mean something very different for Alex or Rob. For example, Helen always seems to link this to the kinds of activities I set her. Alex seems to link it to the time he has to do things. Rob to the clarity of my explanations. He hates it when he doesn't think he understands what he's got to do. He can get very dependent on me and demands a lot of my time. Angus seems to make sense of what I ask him to do when he can relate things back to what he already knows, like our earlier work on local farming. When he can do this he's happy and talks about the lesson being 'easy'. And this reminds me of another thing. When Anna, Jenny and Sanjay talk about the lesson being hard or easy for them they usually link it to their level of enjoyment.*
>
> *Then there are more subtle things I've begun to appreciate like when two or three children all talk about the same bits of the lesson. It's different for different children. For example, we did some work where I wanted the children to empathise with the daily routine of Kenyan villagers having to use hand tools to dig the ground and then to bring the water to the crops in buckets from a long way away. Chris had difficulty with the whole business of empathising whereas Ranjit said the bit about measuring the distance they had to walk to fetch water, by using the map, was hard. Amir just said he couldn't get into it.*
>
> *So what am I learning? The children don't all make sense of the lesson in the same way. So what's new! Then, when they use the same words to describe it, the words can mean different things to each child. I have learnt to stop guessing what they mean and ask them what they mean by it. It's made me much more aware that I shouldn't get complacent. Not all the children will enjoy and get something out of the lessons, some will, some won't. Even when I think it was a really good lesson there will always be some who will think differently. They interpret things in their own way.*

Teachers literally create professional knowledge. Clandinin and Connelly (1995) use a landscape metaphor to describe this. They argue that teachers create and inhabit a professional knowledge landscape, 'composed of at least two kinds of places: the in-classroom place where teachers work with students and the out-of-classroom communal, professional place' (Clandinin 1995: 28). The landscape metaphor is particularly appropriate; like professional knowledge, landscapes evolve and change with time. They are made up of many things that are positioned and interrelated in particular ways. We can get lost in a landscape and need maps to find our way and give our journeying a sense of purpose and direction. Reflections-on-practice in the form of interpreted texts can function as important way-finding maps. As teachers oscillate from one part of the landscape to another, the one behind the classroom door to those professional places with others, reflection-on-practice becomes crucial in order to make sense of the 'dilemma-laden quality of being in both' (Clandinin and Connelly 1995: 5).

Social construction is a theory about how we learn. Based upon the work of Fosnot (1996) we can tentatively establish some principles of learning derived from constructionism.

1. Learning requires skilful self-organisation on the part of the teacher.
2. Disequilibrium facilitates learning and contradictions in particular need to be illuminated, explored and discussed.
3. Reflection-on-practice is the driving force for learning.
4. Reflective conversations within a 'community of teachers' engenders further learning. Dialogue, for example, through learning journals and face-to-face with peers is crucial. In this way 'reality' and 'truth' are accepted insofar as they make sense to the community. Interpretations of teaching and learning thus become regarded as 'taken-as-shared'.
5. Practice moves forward as teachers build cognitive structures, critical thinking frameworks and develop 'big ideas' which help to bring aspects of teaching and learning into an integrated whole. The enabling model upon which this book coheres is an example of such a 'construction'.

The validation of practice

At the heart of our enabling model of making sense of reflections-on-practice are three assumptions. They are that developing our professionality means being able to:

*   justify what it is we claim we know from reflecting-on-practice;
*   justify how far this knowing, which we have personally constructed, is worthwhile;
*   demonstrate the links between improvements in our thinking and our teaching.

When teachers present a claim that, through reflection, their practice has moved forward, they will need to be selective, convincing and criterial. Being selective means that the teacher should carefully choose one aspect of teaching and learning that might be regarded as a good example of improvement. They then have to present their claim in such a way that others might find it convincing. Finally teachers need to specify the criteria that they wish others to use if they are to make valid judgements about the worthiness of the claim. Individual teachers should exercise their right to establish the criteria they believe are appropriate, based on their practice-based knowledge. But they should be prepared to justify them. People who might judge the worthiness of a teacher's claim may not share, undertand or value the teacher's criteria. They may employ criteria of their own. Differences of this kind often lead to misunderstanding and a different perception of the nature and validity of the claim being made. The issue of the nature of the criteria and who owns them is contentious and contested. Who makes the judgement and who has the competency and right to judge the validity of the claim, can also be highly problematic.

There are three main types of validation. They are *critical self-validation*, *peer-group validation* and *public validation* which involves having work accepted for publication. Critical self- validation has been something of a golden thread throughout this book. In this process teachers must be prepared to look for and accept evidence which is supportive, palatable and confirmatory of their feelings and sense of developing self. They also need to avoid turning a blind eye to evidence which challenges and confronts currently held values and practices. A teacher's inability to be open to this kind of threat will affect, and perhaps distort, their understanding of their practice and the context in which it is situated.

Peer-group validation is a complex process with three important differences to critical self-validation. It is a public not a private act. It is enacted in a group rather than done alone. An understanding of group dynamics, of roles and responsibilities is therefore essential. It uses communication with others to bind the process together. Peer-group validation depends for its richness on a group who are willing to share and critique claims that practice has indeed moved forward. Peer groups can usefully be regarded as a community of 'critical friends'. The principle function of such friends is to generate a constructive and yet critical dialogue about the trustworthiness of the claim being made. Critical friends are often hard to find so it is important that the teacher thinks through the attributes of such people.

When acting as a critical friend it is worth considering adopting the disposition of 'reflective scepticism' (McPeck 1990). This means that we suspend, or temporarily reject, the available evidence as sufficient for establishing the truth or 'worthwhileness' of the claim being made. The notion of 'good reasons' is important here. Claims should be based on good reasons. Critical friends need to look out for them as teachers present their claims to know. This requires them to be astute, open-minded and good listeners. Paul (1990) recommends that the process of 'intellectual give-and-take' is used when teachers test out, in a public forum, their claims that 'things are different now'. Dialogical and dialectical thinking are ingredients of this give-and-take. Dialogical thinking refers to, 'thinking that involves dialogue or extended exchange between different points of view' (p. 339). Dialectical thinking refers to 'dialogical thinking conducted in order to test the strengths and weaknesses of opposing points of view' (p. 340).

A illustration: Fragments of teacher talk from peer validation meetings

- I found it difficult to be precise. My claim was huge. A silly claim really, that I had improved communication in school. I didn't really specify where, in what ways and how I know what I know. I didn't back things up with evidence. I don't think I was very convincing so it was no wonder that I felt they took me to the cleaners!

- We wrestled, as a group, with this word evidence and how it could best be used to support my claim that I had developed my classroom questioning skills.

- My claim is that I am better at delegation now than I was this time last year and that this has made me more effective in my job as headteacher. Well I soon appreciated that I was making two claims and not one and that I needed evidence about delegation and effectiveness.

- It's now obvious to me that I can get some evidence to support my claim more easily than other types.

- If I'm claiming that I have improved my listening skills, then why shouldn't anyone believe it!

- The really big problems are communicating what I am claiming to be true clearly and convincingly. The message and the medium are important. From the reactions I got, I obviously failed. Maybe they were never going to accept what I said. If so then we should have agreed to differ. I've learnt that I could have done more, gathered more evidence, done more analysis, more and more. But this isn't the point as I see it. All I wanted from them is some acknowledgement that what I was claiming was indeed reasonable given the evidence and the constraints I was working under.

- The peer group were wonderful. They listened but not for too long. They asked questions but not in a confrontational manner. They allowed me time to think and to reflect on the way the thing was going. They challenged me but did so in a professionally empowering manner. I definitely got a lot from it and I hope they did also. I think there was trust, tolerance and fairness between us. It is these things that I believe are fundamental to any significant educational enterprise.

CHAPTER SIX

Reflection-on-context: Partnership in Practice

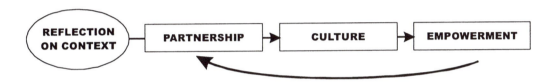

Reflection-on-partnership

Ask most student teachers what makes a 'good' school experience and they will name three key things:

1. their relationship with the class teacher;
2. their relationship with the children;
3. the general school environment and culture.

Put another way, the *context* in which students find themselves is critical and affects how they approach their school experiences, how they make sense of what it means to be an effective teacher and what they learn from the experience. The class teacher, children and the school's culture can 'make or break' many student teachers. Coming to terms with managing the context in which they are teaching is part of the repertoire of skills that inexperienced teachers need to develop. Contexts often range from the very supportive, collegial environments, where the student teacher and class teacher work alongside one another and learn from one another, to less supportive, even hostile environments, where student teachers feel uncomfortable in the class teacher's presence and unwelcome in the school.

Few providers of initial teacher training would wish for their students to find themselves in the latter situation. Indeed there is a requirement on all providers to ensure that schools work 'in partnership' with them. 'The lynchpins of these partnerships are the co-operating teachers, acting as mentors, guiding the "seeing" of student teachers' (Dunne and Bennett 1997: 225). Since 1993 UK Government intervention has made partnership more formalised and systematic

(Nicholls 1997). There is now a requirement that, 'schools are fully and actively involved in the planning and delivery of initial teacher training, as well as in the selection and final assessment of trainees' (DfEE 1998b). The notion of partnership carries with it a resource implication, which generally involves the exchange of professional expertise, training of mentors for school experience, funding for school placements, in-service training related to initiatives such as the Literacy and Numeracy Hours and developing a support network involving teachers, mentors and tutors. One of the most important resource issues is that of the cost of school-based training (Cunnah *et al.* 1997). This is notoriously difficult to determine in an educational context. At its simplest, partnership involves a transfer of funds away from traditional providers of initial teacher training, such as Universities and Colleges of Higher Education, to schools. This financial remuneration is designed to cover the cost of such things as time spent mentoring student teachers (Mardle 1995). But all schools have to weigh up the actual costs of training against any other 'profits' or benefits that such an involvement with traditional providers might bring. In OFSTED (1995b) language these are called 'difficulties' and 'benefits'.

The more informal, non-prescriptive partnership between schools and providers of initial teacher training, which has existed for decades, has now been replaced with explicit terms and agreements which, it might be argued, changes the whole nature of partnership. Some have argued that partnership has had a 'transformative cultural effect' as schools embrace the work of the training of student teachers and make it part of their professional life (Cunnah *et al.* 1997). But Fowler (1997) reminds us of the difference between the espoused benefits and the reality of implementation.

> The understanding of true partnership as essentially functionalist, implying the greater good for all, the sharing of expertise and an altruistic commitment to a common objective can sometimes become blurred by the pressures associated with resources.
>
> (Fowler 1997: 11)

Some of the fundamental questions with regard to the partnership between schools and traditional providers of initial teacher training are raised by McIntyre and Hagger (1996). The questions are:

1. How clear are the conditions of the partnership: what is expected of the partners in terms of what will be done when, and how, and in relation to what criteria of quality?
2. What division of labour is seen as being appropriate between universities and schools, and as being realistic in terms of each institution's capacity to make effective provision for different kinds of learning experiences?
3. To what extent, and in what ways, is student teachers' work in the two contexts integrated, so that what is done in the university is effectively used in school-based learning, and what is done in each context is effectively questioned in the other?
4. What kinds of constraints limit the realisation in practice of theoretical conceptions of the kinds of partnership which should be operating between schools and universities?

(McIntyre and Hagger 1996: 6–7)

Clearly-defined selection criteria now have to be agreed, which address issues related to the quality of experience to which student teachers are entitled while working in schools. Roles and responsibilities, both of schools and providers, are explicitly stated and, in many instances, a partnership contract is drawn up between provider and school. There is an expectation that schools will demonstrate a whole-school commitment to initial teacher training and welcome student teachers into the full life of the school. Periods of time have to be set aside for observation, discussion and reflection on the student's progress. Mentors must be identified who will undertake training and be responsible for the general welfare and supervision of student teachers while in the school. Formal assessment procedures need to be followed which are both formative (for example using a profiling system) and summative (for example writing final, summary reports). Each provider of initial teacher training is at liberty to set their own school selection criteria to suit particular needs and goals. This is generally agreed in partnership with schools through committee structures and meetings. Having once established the selection criteria, providers are required to ensure that all schools meet them. The DfEE clearly states, 'where partnership schools fall short of the selection criteria set, providers must demonstrate that extra support will be provided to ensure that the training provided is of a high standard' (DfEE 1998b: 137).

There is an agreement between traditional providers and schools that student experiences will be monitored carefully and that steps will be taken to ensure that partnership incorporates a common understanding of the needs and entitlement of all student teachers. The rhetoric seems clear on this (DfE 1992b, 1993b). The Government's official rationale for the establishment of partnerships was couched in the language of improving the quality of provision.

So why, in reality, and despite Government legislation, do some student teachers find themselves in a teaching context which is unsupportive and one that appears not to facilitate their learning? Could it be that the benefits of partnership do not really exist in practice? (Glover and Mardle 1996). Certainly in the mid-1990s concerns were being raised. Some reports framed these as 'barriers to the successful evolution of partnership' (McIntyre and Hagger 1996). Barriers, for example, included;

> ... schools' perceptions that they were not treated as equals, that they were not adequately funded, and that they were neglected by the HEI (Higher Education Institution) especially in coping with marginal students. Schools wanted both to be consulted and to have the freedom for College guidelines ... to be interpreted in the light of school needs.
>
> (p. 152)

Concerns such as these raise questions about the un/equal nature of the partnership arrangements. McIntyre and Hagger (1996) caricature an unequal partnership thus:

> ... what seems generally to be happening is that HEI's, preferably taking account of the views of schools, specify requirements and provide some financial resources and whatever limited support they feel they can promise. The schools get on as best they can with the more or less clearly specified task of teacher training ... From this perspective, then, the partnership looks basically to be one of the universities paying schools to train teachers.
>
> (p. 153)

On reflection, the principle and process of partnership was becoming understood and experienced, in the mid-1990s, in very different ways. Some of these were 'uneasy partnerships' (Taylor 1997). Those involved had to think through their commitment to the concept of school-based training, to what might constitute effective communication between all the parties involved, the likely costs that would be incurred and address the sincerely felt need for quality time to do the job properly (Campbell and Kane 1996). Responsibilities for teacher training were being shifted across to schools. One of the unresolved issues concerned the location of the real power base and whether or not there was an equivalent transfer of power from higher education to schools.

Some models of partnership

Given this scenario it is not surprising that different 'models' of partnership began to emerge which were a blend of responses to central Government directives and accommodation to local conditions. Furlong *et al.* (1996) identified three 'ideal typical' models of partnership that had started to emerge by 1995. They called them 'collaborative', 'HEI-led' and 'separatist' partnership models. Although in reality local provision blurred the edges between the models, evidence for them as distinctive types was available. They argue that the models occupied the 'middle ground' between the traditional HEI-based schemes of 1992 on the one hand, and the School Centred Initial Teacher Training Schemes (SCITTs) on the other. The latter is school-led provision where consortia of schools, rather than higher education institutions, receive an income and provide some or all of the training. The differences between the models is shown in Table 6.1.

In the collaborative model, teachers and staff from higher education work and plan together on a regular basis. The student experience is one where they are exposed to different forms of knowledge which come from school and from higher education.

> Students are expected and encouraged to use what they learn in school to critique what they learn within the HEI and vice versa. It is through this dialectic that they are expected to build up their own body of professional knowledge
>
> (Furlong *et al.* 1996: 44)

The HEI-led model is very different. Here partnership is conceived as schools providing appropriate learning opportunities for students as defined and monitored by HEI staff. In the separatist model, schools and HEIs are viewed as having;

> ... separate and complementary responsibilities but where there is no systematic attempt to bring these two dimensions into dialogue. In other words there is partnership but not necessarily integration in the course; integration is something that the students themselves have to achieve.
>
> (p. 47)

This model is a pragmatic response to limited resources. With financial pressures on HEIs leading to reduced numbers of school visits by tutors, a separatist model with teachers taking greater responsibility for student development in agreed areas, was seen as a cheaper alternative to the other models of partnership. However in the majority of courses reviewed by Furlong *et al.*, the HEI-led model of partnership dominated. One of the fundamental reasons for this was the feeling that this model was a way of managing school-based student teacher experience so that it achieved what those in higher education regarded as effective training. HEI leadership in this was seen to be essential.

Table 6.1 Ideal models of partnership (Furlong et al. *1996)*

Key characteristics	Collaborative partnership model	HEI-led partnership model	Separatist partnership model
Planning	Emphasis on giving all tutors and teachers opportunities to work together in small groups	HEI-led with at most some consultation of small group of teachers	Broad planning of structure with agreed areas of responsibility
HEI visits to school	Collaborative to discuss professional issues together	Strong emphasis on quality control; monitoring that school is delivering agreed learning opportunities	Very few or none
Documentation	Codifies emerging collaborative practice	Strongly emphasised, defining tasks for schools	Strongly emphasised, defining areas of responsibility.
Content	Schools and HEI recognise legitimacy and differences of each others' contribution to an ongoing dialogue	HEI defines what students should learn in school	Separate knowledge domains, no opportunities for dialogue
Mentoring	Defined as giving students access to teachers' professional knowledge – mentor 'training' as professional development, learning to articulate embedded knowledge	Mentors trained to deliver what course defines as necessary	Mentoring comes from knowledge base of school
Assessment	Collaborative, based on triangulation	HEI-led and defined	School responsible for teaching assessment
Contractual relationship	Negotiated, personal	Directive with lists of tasks and responsibilities	Legalistic, finance led with discrete areas of responsibility
Legitimation	Commitment to value of collaboration in initial teacher education	Acceptance of HEI-defined principles of initial teacher education	Either principled commitment to role of school or pragmatic due to limited resources

This raises a host of issues principally about power relationships, what constitutes quality provision, the nature of professional development and pragmatics. Lee and Wilkes (1996) try to be positive about partnership when they state that, 'what is important is to have a vision of change which will improve the quality of students' experience, and encourage professional development of both tutors and teachers involved in new partnerships' (p. 110).

'Why do you offer student teachers a placement in your school?'

Generally speaking, there is both a principled and a pragmatic response given by many teachers and headteachers to this question. The principled response is related to the nurturing of the next generation of teachers, to providing positive and experienced role models and to the school being an integral part of the training of teachers. The pragmatic response is related to the notion that student teachers are 'another pair of hands' and that their presence in school 'releases' the class teacher to deal with other school and/or curriculum matters. This, in practice, means that those teachers who have year group, whole-school or curriculum responsibilities and who are deemed to require 'time off' to focus on these aspects of their role, are frequently given students to take over the teaching and management of the class. For this reason, final year students are always popular with schools and there is often an assumption that they will be independent and require little or no support and feedback.

Another, rarely acknowledged, reason given for placing students in particular classes and with particular teachers, has a somewhat spurious professional justification. This relates to the use of student teachers as role models for weaker teachers who may be functioning in a less competent way than headteachers would like. In this instance, the children's welfare and education are clearly at the heart of the decision-making process but the student teacher's needs will almost certainly be neglected, leaving the student teacher often feeling isolated and unsupported. There is also a political link here: schools need to know that there is a return on their investment. Time is precious, teachers have full and busy working lives, classes are often large and stress levels high. Changes to the National Curriculum, impending OFSTED inspections and reports, the adminstering of Standard Assessment Tasks (SATs) and the publication of league tables, among other things, mean that student teachers are part of a much wider, complex educational context. Headteachers see opportunities to save on tightly squeezed budgets by using student teachers as supply cover when other members of staff are absent through illness or are attending courses. Additionally, few teachers want to be faced with a 'weak' student or with a student who is known to require higher levels of support than others.

There is therefore a political assumption that all schools appreciate the purpose and value of having student teachers in school. 'High status, high standards' (DfEE 1998b) now trips off the tongue and there is often a complacent attitude that the political definition of 'partnership' as stated in Circular 4/98 is mutually supported and understood by providers and schools alike. In reality there is a danger that schools will resist the imposition of roles and responsibilities by providers and argue that the very gesture of offering a placement to student teachers should be gratefully accepted. Few providers are in the enviable position of being offered so many placements that they can 'pick and choose'. This therefore means that schools, in practice, hold the trump card. Whatever model of partnership emerges locally, the bottom line is that partnership depends upon the recruitment of a sufficient number of good schools, willing to take on the role of student supervision and within a reasonable travelling distance from the HEI. Until the

Government make it a requirement that all schools must form a partnership with a provider of initial teacher training (and this by its very nature would signify compliance rather than collaboration) there will always be students who find themselves in schools where pragmatic reasons have justified their presence rather than principled ones.

This is the nightmare scenario for all school experience placement coordinators within higher education. Partnership agreements and quality assurance procedures dominate much of their workload and negative reports relating to student experiences in schools can lead to feelings of frustration. The situation is further exacerbated by the Government's requirement that providers of initial teacher training 'de-select' schools who do not meet selection criteria and where providers cannot guarantee extra support. However understandable this may be, in reality providers are then faced with a dilemma. Professionally speaking, only schools able to offer high-quality experiences should be considered for the placement of students. Pragmatically, there are often too many student teachers to place in schools and not enough schools in which to place them! Since providers guarantee students a suitable placement as part of their course, this leaves many institutions in a catch 22 situation. Add to this inspection visits to HEIs from OFSTED, keen to assess quality assurance procedures and to discuss student experiences in partnership schools, and the situation becomes more problematic. Yet, despite all these issues, it might be argued that no amount of careful monitoring and selection can guarantee that schools will adopt an appropriately professional stance when accepting students. So, in reality, perhaps student teachers should be prepared for a diversity of contexts where both professional and pragmatic influences affect the quality of their experience while in school.

It is not surprising therefore that, given the above, student teachers can feel either liberated or constrained by the school context in which they find themselves. From the outset students often have a *feeling* about a school. After just one visit many are able to offer vivid descriptions of the school's atmosphere, the relationships between staff, the ethos, the response from the children, attitudes, expectations and so forth. These things are part of the school's culture. The descriptions may be highly idiosyncratic and perhaps skewed, but they nevertheless impact on the student's feelings of self-worth, capability and enthusiasm. One of the most pervasive influences on the quality of teachers' work is the school's culture. Reflection-on-practice means more than simply reflecting on individual work in the classroom; it also means reflecting on practice in a context. The context is the school which is part of a wider socio-cultural and politico-economic 'system'. We should not only reflect-on-practice but also reflect on the context in which practice is embedded. A key question here is, 'Does immersion in a particular school culture provide the most appropriate learning experience for student teachers?'

Reflections-on-context: Jo's first morning in school

The following extract is taken from a journal of a final year primary student named Jo, who reflects on the difference between her third and fourth year school experience. She writes an insightful account of the impact the school's culture had upon her experience and how this affected her ability to reflect positively on her developing professionality. She begins with her recollections of her first morning in a primary school during her third year of teacher training.

From the moment I entered the school I felt uneasy. No one welcomed me as I arrived and I was left wondering whether I was even expected. When I eventually found someone to speak to I was greeted with the words, 'Oh, so you're the student? I think you're with Mrs S in Year 4'. This was not reassuring and, to make matters worse, on entering the classroom, I was met by a very frustrated, rather impatient teacher who announced, in no uncertain terms, that she was too busy to deal with me at the moment and could I make myself useful by taking the children's chairs off the tables because the cleaner had left them there overnight! Needless to say this was not the introduction that I had anticipated, but I wanted to remain positive and so waited for the opportunity to speak with her at another time. The bell rang. Children rushed into the classroom, seemingly oblivious to my presence, and pushed past each other to their seats. The noise level was high. I tried smiling at a group of children but they just stared at me and then became convulsed in giggles. Things would be fine when the class teacher introduced me, I thought. After all, these children would be my responsibility for the next seven weeks. The teacher shouted, very loudly. I jumped. The children hardly seemed to notice. She shouted again and then proceeded to call the register. Some children listened but others continued to chat. They were instructed to take out their spelling books and then to copy lists of words off the board. Still no introduction. I was standing towards the back of the classroom feeling rather lost.

I decided to move around the room and see if any of the children needed help. One child asked who I was and so I quietly explained that I was going to be their teacher for a few weeks and that I was really looking forward to working in their class. At this point another child, some distance away from me, asked in a loud voice, 'Who are you?' Feeling embarrassed at the sea of faces that turned to stare, I looked to the class teacher for support. 'Oh, yes children', she started, 'this is the student who's joining us for a while. Say hello everyone'. My heart sank. I was announced as 'the student'. I had no name and little status. Any chance of respect from the children or of feeling on equal terms with the class teacher quickly disappeared. I felt dejected and disillusioned and this was just 30 minutes into the school experience!

Jo must have wondered at this point why she had been accepted into the school and why she had been placed in this particular class. Her personal reaction was to feel rejected and unwanted but her professional reaction was to look for reasons why today may be stressful for the teacher and why she ought to give things time before passing judgement. She continues with her account describing the structured class routines and the way she tried to 'make herself useful and unobtrusive' until the point of playtime when the bell rings. She continues,

On hearing the bell there was a resounding, 'Yes!' from the whole class, a rummaging in desks for crisps and snacks and then a charge for the door. The class teacher sighed and then grabbed her coat announcing, 'Monday's playground duty. Make yourself a coffee. It's Maths after play.' With that she disappeared. I was left wondering what to do. A child, who was searching ardently for something in a pile of coats that were strewn around the floor, asked politely if I knew where the staffroom was. I did not. As if recognising my hopelessness, he offered to escort me there and then proceeded to tell me that Mrs S was the deputy head and a very busy lady who didn't usually have time to talk to visitors. I think this was meant to reassure me that I was not an excep-

tion to the rule! At least I felt that I had found a perceptive child who sensed a need to talk to me and help me find a way to another part of the school. This in itself comforted me. I was shown to a staffroom where teachers were busily making cups of coffee, engaging in conversation and thumbing through green sheets. I walked in and looked rather apprehensively around. No one seemed to notice me. I tried to catch someone's eye but they all seemed rather elusive! Should I help myself to a coffee, sit down, start a conversation or what? I searched for a face to relate to and then, when I had almost given up hope, a young woman smiled at me and walked over. 'You're looking a little lost', she said. 'Are you a student?' It must be written all over my face, I thought.

I introduced myself and she explained that she was a classroom assistant and general dogsbody! She showed me the cupboard where mugs were kept and made me a coffee. A light in the darkness, I thought, albeit a flicker. Then, just as I felt that I was getting somewhere, two windswept little faces arrived at the staffroom door and announced that it had started raining and so Mrs S was going to blow the whistle! A groan went up from the assembled staff, mugs, still half-full, were deposited beside the sink and everyone made a move back to their classroom. My one opportunity to make some sense of what was happening had gone.

Jo's perception of the school's culture is worsening. She has only received a positive response to her presence in school from two people, one a child, one a non-teaching member of staff. She has no idea who the headteacher is or whether there is a student mentor in the school. The situation is not looking promising yet she has to reassure herself that this is only a few hours into the practice and perhaps not an ideal time to assess what her prospects are in terms of a rewarding and valuable school experience. After eventually finding her way back to the classroom her account continues.

Some children were finishing packets of crisps, others were sprawled across tables. The noise level was high but fortunately no children appeared to be arguing or looking for trouble. There was no sign of Mrs S. I wished I hadn't returned so early. The children ignored me and continued their conversations. I felt as though I should be telling them to sit down and to get on with some work but I didn't think that this was appropriate at the present time. I fumbled in my bag as though looking for a file or something. Perhaps, at wet playtime, the children always amused themselves. Perhaps Mrs S needed a comfort break. I started to write notes, any notes, just to look busy! One child fell off his chair. I moved towards him but he leapt up and pretended that he really wasn't hurt at all. Obviously he did not want me interfering.

Another child approached me and said that I had nice hair and what was my name and did I like her new shoes? I smiled and said that I thought her shoes were lovely and asked her her name. At this point she settled very comfortably on a chair next to me and proceeded to tell me everything about herself, her family, her friends (who were sometimes mean to her but usually nice), her pet dog called 'Wolf' and her favourite singer. A group formed around me and quickly fought for my attention as more and more personal information was thrust at me. Children seemed to be swarming from all directions and pushing to get closer. Hot breath, still sweetly scented with pickled onion crisps, began to stifle me and so I awkwardly surfaced from amidst the group and suggested that I have a look at their work on the walls. Bad move. As I

> *glanced around there was an obvious lack of attention paid to displaying the children's work and those displays that did exist looked highly dated with faded backing paper and work peeling at the edges where shoulders had been systematically rubbed against it. The children looked nonplussed and quickly changed the conversation back to far more important issues such as the character assassination of Jamie who, to his credit, stood his ground defiantly beside me and denied all accusations made against him. Then, just as I was wondering what my next move was, an ear-piercing shout of 'Sit down now!' reverberated around the room. To my surprise the children actually moved back to their seats and looked almost ready to do some work. The Maths lesson began.*

A lively class without a doubt. Jo might describe them as interesting and challenging in one context or overbearing and bewildering in another. Faced with the prospect of teaching in the school for seven weeks she has to find a way to adjust to and manage her situation to the best of her ability. The current state of affairs suggests that she has received little or no recognition and that everyone is too busy to pay her any attention. The tightly structured lessons, which she goes on to describe, with children sat in rows and working from textbooks, bear no resemblance to lessons that she has previously witnessed or taught, where children have been actively engaged in group tasks, working towards common goals, sharing ideas, respecting one another's opinion and generally being responsive to the learning environment.

Jo believes there is a conflict in her values. The conflict is between her perception of what school and classroom life should be about and in what she has actually experienced in school A. She feels the school's culture is not an empowering one because, although the children eventaully warm to her and she works hard to build a relationship with them, there is no support given by members of the teaching staff. The headteacher has no involvement in her progress. The named mentor rarely observes lessons and the class teacher, eventually recognising Jo's ability to teach, leaves her to manage the class alone while she pursues her duties as deputy head. This is a very difficult culture in which to be a student teacher and, not surprisingly, affects the way Jo feels about herself and about the value placed on her contribution to teaching within the school.

A visiting tutor would probably be alarmed at the situation, take steps to try to support the student and address the sensitive issues. How tutors see their role when supervising students in school is crucial here (Lee and Wilkes 1996). Quality support is clearly what Jo needs at this time. For teachers this means knowing how they might best help the student; intuitive and 'gut' reactions may not be an appropriate response from them (Hagger *et al.* 1995). It is not hard to imagine how difficult it would have been for Jo to engage in a reflective conversation about her teaching when she was experiencing such negative feelings. In her journal she describes how she became 'defensive, sensitive to criticism' and believed that any pupil misbehaviour was due to her 'inept performance'. She writes of feeling 'used' within the school and receiving 'no encouragement or positive feedback'.

The fact that the teacher feels able to leave her class in Jo's hands does not alleviate her diminishing self-confidence. Her previous, relatively high, self-esteem is threatened and any reflective conversation with a visiting tutor, or other school staff member would need to be handled with great care to avoid making matters worse. An empowering conversation would help Jo to work with her negativities and feelings of low self-esteem. Some appropriate kinds of support would help restore Jo's confidence, help her think more positively and enable her to reappraise or reaffirm the validity of her own values. This does not happen overnight and the work of Borko and Mayfield (1995) does not give us grounds for a great deal of optimism. In their work of the influence on student teacher learning of 'cooperating' teachers and university staff they concluded that interactions with supervisors were too rushed and based upon insufficient data about the student's teaching. One consequence of this is that students come to have low expectations about what they might get out of reflective conversations with their supervisors.

Those who work with students need to address how far there is a 'shared desire to maximise comfort and minimise risks during teaching practices' (Dunne and Bennett 1997: 226). Challenge with support are the hallmarks of learning from reflection-on-practice presented in this book; challenge without support can be destructive. Support without challenge is about comfort. Always being comfortable can lead to blindness, a professional state in which the teacher misses and dismisses opportunities to improve their practice and the quality of the learning experiences of their pupils.

Reflection-on-context: Jo's experience in another school

Jo is given the opportunity to restore her confidence, put things in perspective and develop her skills in a different school ten months later when she embarks on her fourth and final school experience. Once again her journal writing provides us with a vivid portrait of School B. Her initial thoughts about her forthcoming practice are thus. Jo writes;

As I nervously approached the reception desk a friendly face looked up from a computer screen and greeted me with a smile. 'You must be Jo', she said, 'I'm Janet, the school secretary. Mr Peters asked me to take care of you while he sees a parent. Would you like a coffee?' I was taken to the staffroom and offered a seat. As the secretary made me a cup of coffee she chatted away and made me feel extremely comfortable. Several members of staff passed through the staffroom on their way to the classroom and, each time, I was introduced by Janet and engaged in a short conversation. People seemed genuinely keen to speak and to make me feel welcome. After five minutes the door opened again and a bustling gentleman appeared with his hand outstretched. 'Jo', he beamed, 'Pleased to meet you. Come on through to my office. Mrs Willliams will join us just as soon as she has set the hall up for assembly.'

He took me into a warmly furnished room with children's pictures on the walls. One caught my eye. A very round, red-faced little man with spectacles and bushy eyebrows had been carefully drawn and painted in bright colours. Underneath were the words, 'To Mr Peters. I think you are very nise. Love Emma.' For an instant I recalled the fact that I had not even seen the inside of the headteacher's room in school A. This experience was so overwhelmingly different that it was almost unnerving. As I was invited to sit down Mr Peters handed me a package with a school brochure and 'student information pack' inside. He asked me to find time to read through it and to see him at any time if I needed clarification on the contents.

At this point, Mrs Williams knocked on the door and came in. She was immediately invited to sit down and to join in the conversation. This was my class teacher who would be responsible for me whilst I was in school. Mr Peters continued, 'Mrs Williams is our deputy head ...' The words went through me like a knife. Not again. Not another deputy head I thought. Never any time to talk, over worked, and always stressed out! It was a dreadful image to have but unfortunately that had always been my experience. Was the bubble about to burst?

He continued. 'She is our school mentor and takes care of all students in school. Mrs Williams will work out a programme with you that gives you time to get to know the children before taking over the class. She'll check your planning and observe your teaching every week so that we make sure all the curriculum subjects are covered.'

Things looked more promising and, as I followed a chatty Mrs Williams to the class-room a few minutes later, I felt an immense wave of relief wash over me. Perhaps this was my lucky day.

Jo's account reflects a very positive and welcoming first impression which suggests that the school is well prepared for students and appreciates the need to make them feel valued. She finds herself in a context which is understanding and supportive of her needs. The fact that senior members of staff had taken time to talk to her and explain the situation to her made her feel appreciated. The procedures that were in place for monitoring and assessing her progress were structured and formalised which meant that she was likely to receive feedback on a regular basis and have the opportunity to reflect on key issues with her class teacher. Her planning would be checked and her lessons observed so that she could identify areas that needed improving and take steps to move her practice forward. The fact that her teacher was also the deputy head concerned her, but she was reassured by knowing that set periods of time were allocated to her for discussing her progress.

As Jo entered the Year 3 classroom, she recalls her perceptions.

The classroom was bright and colourful. Every inch of wall space seemed to boast children's work, display tables were full of interesting objects and the children's desks were neatly arranged in groups. There was space to move around comfortably, a book corner with soft cushions on the floor and an achievements chart on the wall. I picked out some of the names. 'Ben, for being kind to Jodie', 'Sophie, for working sensibly with Darren', 'Paul, for helping Mrs Murray', 'Lucy, for trying extra hard'. I felt comfortable in the room. Mrs Williams had placed a seat next to her desk ready for me and a file with her medium-term planning in it for me to look through while she pre-pared for the children to come in. As she busied herself around the room, she continued to chat about the children, the way she had grouped them and her general expectations. She was obviously a highly committed teacher who took pride in her classroom and who spoke very warmly about her pupils.

When the bell rang I almost expected little angels to walk serenely through the door but, in fact, it was a boisterous, noisy bunch who scrambled in and made for their desks. As they passed me several children said 'hello' and asked if I was their new teacher, Miss Harris. I smiled and said that I was and that I would be working with Mrs Williams until the Easter holidays. They seemed happy with that. Mrs Williams raised one hand in the air and, as if by magic, a hush fell over the classroom. All the children listened as she introduced me and explained how much the children had been looking forward to meeting me. Then, as she marked the register, the children each said their name and told me one thing about themselves. It was a planned and rehearsed introduction with giggles from some of the class and nudges from others as children took their turn. A cheeky comment alerted me to the class clown and an almost inaudible whisper to the shy child by my side.

The impression that it made on me was lasting. The children's individual characters started to shine through and I found myself warming to them immediately. There had been an obvious effort on the part of Mrs Williams to prepare my path and to help the children accept me. She had organised my work for the morning and managed things so that I would meet each group before the end of my first day. During breaks she encouraged me to accompany her to the staffroom and to meet other members of staff. As the day progressed I was able to make reflective notes, collect together copies of planning sheets and become familiar with her routines. It was the start of a promising eight weeks.

Jo's frame of mind was changing. The negative experiences that she associated with her previous school placement were gradually being challenged and the possibility of an improvement in her self-esteem and practice now seemed likely. In subsequent discussions with her it became evident that she learned a great deal from reflecting on her experiences in both schools, apart from the obvious, 'all schools are different'.

Returning to the issues of principle and pragmatism mentioned earlier, we could say that school A had a very different agenda for offering student placements than school B. In school A it could be argued that Jo was not seen as an 'emerging' teacher, who needed support and encouragement, but as an experienced professional who should know what to do and who would have to get on with it. Having clearly specified standards to attain (DfEE 1998b) did little to help her reflect in a reasoned way and she became convinced that she was achieving none of her targets.

In direct contrast was her experience in a highly supportive environment, school B, where her status as a student teacher (rather than a fully qualified, experienced teacher) was understood and accepted and where a professional stance was adopted from the outset. This gradually improved her low self-esteem and began to help her adopt a new reflective posture based on looking for what was positive and rewarding in her practice and nourishing this, rather than focusing only on that which was 'going wrong' and demoralising her. In this context she was able to put mistakes into perspective and to identify where aspects of her practice could be improved. She could engage in meaningful discussions with her teacher that were non-threatening and constructive. This example illustrates, not only the need for a shared understanding about the process of learning as a student teacher, but also the significance of acknowledging that we do not all hold the same professional values and even if we did we might try to live them out in different ways. Where a teacher's values conflict with a student's own espoused values and values-in-action, tensions can emerge. Given this scenario, student teachers generally opt for one of the following:

(a) *A rejection of their own values:* Where this is the case the student may 'adopt' the values of the class teacher for the duration of the school experience. Many students take this option 'for a quiet life', to try to ensure that the teacher will approve of their approach to teaching and to give themselves a chance of passing the practice.

(b) *A rejection of the teacher's values:* This normally occurs where students feel unable to use the teacher as a role model and dislike the way that the children are treated. It requires considerable confidence, maturity and strength and brings with it the possibility of disapproval, rejection and a failed school experience.

(c) *A compromise on values:* Students who compromise have usually reflected on the notion that rarely do two individuals share all the same values and that, from a professional point of view, an acceptance of a diversity of values is often a necessity and reality when work-ing in school. These students respect some of the teacher's values while maintaining some of their own values. They aim to achieve a working synthesis for the time that they are in school. Each option carries with it certain implications and these need to be fully appreci-ated by the student.

The articulation of individual and collective values and the culture of a school are inextrica-bly linked. When student teachers 'take over' a class they inevitably convey certain intended and unintended values to the children and thereby influence the learning culture within the classroom. Experienced teachers, when observing the impact of a student's presence on the culture of their classroom, can, for example, feel threatened or reassured. Where the develop-ing culture is conducive to effective learning there is often little or no need to challenge the student teacher's practice. But where a teacher feels that the 'new approach' inhibits learning and perhaps begins to undermine the teacher's good work, there is an increased possibility that the student's practice will be questioned. This may be perceived by students as a direct attack on their values and, as such, brings with it the likelihood of disillusionment or disappointment. At worst, this might lead to confrontation but, at best, it could provide an opportunity to engage in a dialogue about the reasons for adopting certain approaches to teaching and managing the class in particular ways. In the ideal partnership, student teachers are encouraged to put their values into practice, to justify them and to reflect on the appropriateness of matching means to educational ends. So if, for example, a student teacher valued the notion of cooperation and collaboration, which in practice implies group work with shared goals, it would be profession-ally rewarding for the student to have the opportunity to try this out. But, if it means that this move might change the learning culture in the classroom because, for example, the class teacher does not see the value of group work and prefers whole-class teaching with children sat in rows, it might be professionally prudent for the student to maintain the existing system.

Taken one step further it becomes evident how each of these two scenarios may impact on the student teacher's experiences and on their perceptions of self. Working within a culture where the student and teacher's values are clearly very different can lead to tension and frustra-tion (see Chapter 4). Student teachers need to reflect on this situation, to understand the con-straints that face them, learn to work within them or to sensitively and constructively question and challenge them. Where these are not seen by the student as viable options, students may feel pressure to demonstrate that they can reproduce and sustain the existing culture, to conform or withdraw from the situation altogether. Students are sometimes in an unenviable situation, caught between the pressures to conform to the culture of the host school while, at the same time, being encouraged to critically reflect on their school experiences by their HEI tu-tors. Campbell and Kane (1996) summarise many of the pertinent issues thus:

> If the culture in school does not engender critical appraisal and reflection, and if, as we believe, teachers themselves find reflection difficult, how can mentors stimulate reflection amongst students? There are many aspects of primary school culture which work against the development of critical reflection on practice: time and space in which to actually reflect ... the value of reflection is often diminished by the need to conform to the latest DfE initiative ... the pressure by inhabitants to socialise new recruits into existing culture and norms (despite an awareness of the dangers of cloning, mentors still referred to students as 'fitting in' at school); the collaborative ethos set up in many schools that encourages conformity rather than conflict.
>
> (Campbell and Kane 1996: 28)

In some cases students can indeed live out values associated with a different learning culture to the one that exists within the class. It is not unknown for teachers to change their own practice as a consequence of seeing student teachers put their different values into action. Indeed, in the true spirit of partnership, the relationship between student and class teacher might usefully be seen as one of mutual growth and learning, where both parties reflect on their values, their reasons for doing things in particular ways and resolve to make improvements for the benefit of the children.

Reflections on the influence of school culture

Our values make us the kind of teacher that we are. We have argued that teachers should make sincere and deliberate attempts to live them out in their teaching; we have also made the point that this is not always possible. One of the major influences here is the school's culture. We should not only reflect on our teaching but on the particular culture within which it is embedded. School culture serves to liberate and constrain us; it provides opportunities for achieving satisfaction, personal renewal and collective regeneration. The school's culture can also stifle, suffocate, marginalise and silence us. Critical reflection questions and challenges those things that disempower and demoralise us.

School culture is a vast field of inquiry and a complex phenomenon, but an understanding of it is important if we are committed to improving teaching and learning through reflection. It impacts greatly on what we think, feel and do in school. It affects our competence and confidence (Wu 1998). It is an appropriate focus for reflection. Chittenden (1993) sets the scene.

> A central feature of school culture is the interpersonal sharing of special experiences and values. Schools have an important contribution to make and a responsibility to clarify and coordinate the various cultural elements because they espouse, either directly or indirectly, a composite of values, philosophy and ideologies which should educate a student intellectually and socially. As an organisation, the various groups in the school try to operationalise the group's values. This means that they are turned into tangible outcomes which attempt to develop coherence and identity.
>
> (Chittenden 1993: 30)

This idea that a school's culture is a 'composite of values' is examined in the work of Wu (1998) who researched the impact of school cultures on the competence of newly qualified teachers. As part of his work with 21 British secondary schools he invited a number of teachers to reflect on and articulate their understandings of the term school culture. The following examples help to place Jo's experiences in schools A and B in a broader context.

(a) A deputy head:

> *We believe that everyone in the school has the right to be treated as an individual and with respect. We value achievements of every kind, academic and non-academic. We believe that everyone in this school should have an equal opportunity to achieve their potential ... We expect everyone to set a good example, work hard and give of their best.*
>
> (Wu 1998: 226)

(b) An experienced class teacher:

What I like about this school's culture is that staff very much care for the children. Above all else, we try to look after every child individually and try to see if we can make every child's life better either academically or from the problems they have got.

(Wu 1998: 230)

(c) A deputy head:

I think the role of the senior management is probably the most significant thing. Whatever we do concerning education and management in the school will affect all the teaching and learning activities, and affect the culture. The senior management at the school are all in the public arena. We are the people who generally monitor educational quality, who work with the community on the school's behalf, who meet the parents … who stand on the stage and talk to large groups of people. So what we stand for is particularly important for the culture.

(Wu 1998: 231)

(d) A deputy head:

I think it is a very valuable point that you want your newly qualified teachers (NQTs) to quickly imbibe your culture and subscribe to it. It is not enough for them just to know it. They have got to be part of it and be developing it, because school culture is made up of the people at the school. It is not a piece of paper that you read and throw away. School culture is the sum total of all the people that are there, hopefully with the common vision pulling in the same direction. What you want of an NQT is somebody who comes along, subscribes to that culture and makes some input into it, actually contributes to its development, not just simply receives it.

(Wu 1998: 243)

Each of these reflections illustrate, in part, different aspects of the complex whole that makes up the phenomenon called school culture. Within one school there may be groups who represent particular sub-cultures. Sometimes these are given names such as the 'management', the 'workers', the 'old guard', the 'young turks', the 'liberals', 'trendies', 'reactionaries', 'subversives', 'resistors' 'saboteurs', and the like. In (a) above the teacher's reflections begin to say something about an 'achievement culture' (Pheysey 1993). Teachers are committed to their work; they are motivated professionals and want their pupils to achieve. In cultures such as this work pressures are always great. In (b), the teacher's reflections begin to describe the characteristics of a 'support culture' where mutual support, teamwork, collegiality and caring for each other are important features. In (c), the teacher alludes to some of the attributes of what Pheysey (1993) calls a 'power culture'. The senior management group is a clear driving force and one which monitors standards. A strong sense of power, managerial control and responsibility begins to emerge from this transcript. Finally, in example (d), the teacher's reflections contain elements of 'role culture'. The deputy head sketches out her perceived role for NQTs in the school. Expectations are articulated together with roles and responsibilities.

Re-seeing Jo's accounts

Reflection-on-context requires the teacher to be skilful at 'noticing'. This is the precursor to making sense of all those things that impinge upon the nature and quality of teaching and learning in the classroom. The teacher needs to notice what is going on in school before reflection can take place. Notice the major events, the trends, dilemmas, extremes, unusual things, the disruptions, routines, subtleties and interdependencies. If these are noticed we have a chance to understand them. Jo's noticing skills were good: she was beginning to describe each school's 'personality' and 'spirit'. These are words often linked with school culture. Tye (1974) explains:

> When an individual visits a school for the first time, he develops, almost immediately, a feeling about the school. This feeling is shaped by what he views. The hallways are empty, or they are bubbling with noise. Students sit quietly at desks, or they move about in various informal arrangements. Expressions are solemn, or they are soft, supporting and questioning. Room and hallway environments are stark, or there is a profusion of children's work, exhibits and plant and animal life. These factors and many more give each school a personality, a spirit, a culture.
>
> (Tye 1974: 20)

When we reflect on practice we should appreciate that there is a dynamic relationship between teacher/s and school culture. Reflecting on the interplay between the two helps the teacher to clarify their feelings about and attitudes towards the school as a workplace. It also helps them realise the reciprocal nature of the impact that the culture of the school exerts on them and they on it. Jo's reflective commentaries begin to illustrate the first part of this; Brown's work (1995) takes us further. He describes nine aspects of organisational culture. Teachers play a part in forming and transforming each one. In turn, each aspect influences what we think, feel and do and determines our individual professional identities. They are:

- *Artefacts:* These adorn the built environment. They are the most visible and superficial manifestations of a school's culture. For example, displays and notices in the school's entrance can reflect how open and welcoming a school is perceived to be.
- *Language in the form of jokes, metaphors, stories, myths and legends:* What teachers say and how they say it tells us a lot about the culture of the school. For example, the use of 'we' instead of 'I' conveys messages about teamwork, collegiality and the way a staff support each other.
- *Behaviour patterns in the form of rites, rituals, ceremonies and celebrations:* These include school fêtes, religious festivities, reunions, parent–teacher outings, fundraising activities and so on. These behaviours serve to reinforce school values and bond people together.
- *Norms of behaviour:* These are the school's rules which make a statement about where it stands in relation to valuing individuals and the provision of quality educational experiences.
- *Heroes:* This refers to the school's characters. They can be relied upon to deliver and 'come up trumps' when the going gets tough. They are motivators, popular and serve the school in a number of supportive ways.

- *Values, beliefs and attitudes*: These are often evident in the school's brochure or prospectus, in the actions of staff and the behaviour of children. For example if a school values honesty, integrity, hard work and equal opportunity these aspects of culture should be evident in the daily life of the school.
- *Ethical codes*: When teachers have to make difficult decisions, for example about pedagogy, differentiation, resource allocation, pupil exclusion, referral, staff welfare, redundancy and early retirement, an ethical code of conduct is needed. Here culture is related to how far the school is seen to act in a fair, just, principled and democratic manner.
- *Basic assumptions*: These incorporate the school's response to such fundamental questions such as, 'What is this school about?', 'What makes it distinctive?', 'What are the givens and the things we take for granted?' Sometimes these assumptions are tacit and need some digging out.
- *History*: A school's culture is not a static thing but changes over time. This can be influenced by both internal and external forces. A new headteacher, a rapid changeover of staff, a fall in the school's roll, a poor OFSTED report, a new Board of Govenors, a successful netball team at a national event, the decision to get together as a cluster of small rural schools, being given some extra computers and so on, can all change the culture of the school over time.

Reflection and empowerment

It is possible for teachers to be reflective but thoroughly uncritical. Teaching experiences can be distorted, self-fulfilling, unchallenged and constraining. For these reasons alone they need to be questioned critically. This was first suggested in Chapter 2 when we set out some different types of reflection. Descriptive and perceptive reflection-on-practice are principally examples of the way teachers reflect on their own competence and professional confidence. Essentially they are examples of seeing and understanding the world from their own perspective. Increasingly receptive, interactive and critical forms of reflection-on-practice place the individual's action in a broader context and bring to the fore the teacher's preparedness and ability to question and challenge the existing order of things. Being a critically reflective practitioner is taking up a questioning disposition towards what teachers and schools actually do and want to do. It is questioning the way individual and collective teacher actions are liberated and constrained by 'local' structures and the wider 'system' within which teachers work. Critical reflection helps teachers to appreciate the nature and power of the forces that constrain them in working towards principled and valued educational outcomes. When coupled with interactive reflection-on-practice, the teacher can work at trying to change these conditions. Greene (1986) captures the essence of this when she uses the phrase 'teachers as challengers'.

The kind of teacher we are is not simply a consequence of personal character, temperament, preference and individual will, important though these things are. The 'discourses, practices and structure of the school' (Hursh 1992: 5) make some things possible because they serve certain interests. They also deny other forms of school organisation and teaching action. Put another way, a school's culture can, for example, be enabling and supportive, can make judgements about what is more or less appropriate action or worthy of attention, can devalue your voice as a practitioner and your contribution to the life of the school. When the latter happens and teachers feel unable to live their values out in their work, they can experience a range of emotions such as frustration, anger, sadness, depression, conflict, pointlessness, being a pawn in a game, detachment, rejection, isolation and powerlessness. Reflection-on-practice offers teachers a chance to work together to re/discover, develop and use the intellectual and emotional power within themselves to try to improve their situation. It has the potential to empower teachers because it is about helping them become more effective agents of educational improvement.

Empowerment through reflection-on-practice is an important outcome. It is also an important characteristic of the discourse in some schools. But there is no one accepted meaning of the term (Johnson and Redmond 1998). For some, empowerment is linked with enhancing human possibility (McLaren 1989). This view sees teachers as confronted with social, political and economic forces which limit what is possible. From the field of feminist studies, the focus is on the empowerment of women (Weiler 1988). Empowerment is about freeing women from oppressive patriarchal regimes, subordinate positions within schools and having their work respected and recognised. Another view of empowerment is offered by writers such as Simpson (1990) and Snyder (1988) where it is equated with notions of professionalism and concerned with granting new respect to teachers by improving the conditions in which they work. In the literature on school leadership, teacher dissatisfaction, participatory decision-making and staff development, for example, expressions of empowerment can be found.

> The use of the term empowerment has become both problematic and paradoxical: problematic because teacher empowerment is becoming yet another slogan of contemporary discourse used for diverse purposes and possessing a variety of meanings; paradoxical because the meanings and 'blueprints' for teacher empowerment have escaped the meaning systems and social actions of the teachers in which they are embedded.
>
> (Melenyzer 1991: 6)

This raises two fundamental questions. The first is, 'So what does empowerment mean to teachers?' For some, their experience is that empowerment is something of a commodity. It is bestowed on or witheld from them: if you have it you are empowered. If not then you are disempowered. Becoming empowered is unproblematic; it is rather like being a passive recipient of a magic potion which can dupe you into thinking that, being empowered happens overnight, and all of a sudden you have a greater sense of control over your professional life and powers of self-determination. If empowerment is seen as something bestowed upon teachers by those people who have it to give, rather than acquired through struggle and negotiation, then it might be better to regard it as just another form of control and oppression. For other teachers, empowerment has come to be known as a learning process when options that add value to the quality of teaching and learning are opened up, seized and acted on. Viewed in this way, empowerment is not an either/or condition, nor is it a commodity. It is a dynamic individual and collective state which is time and context dependent: empowerment is enabling (Garman 1995).

The second key question is, 'What do empowered teachers do?' In her work on teacher empowerment with 40 middle school teachers in the USA, Melenyzer (1991) concluded that empowered teachers:

- assumed leadership roles and sought opportunities to share leadership with other teachers;
- shared in making decisions that affected their lives at school;
- actively expanded their own knowledge base and shared knowledge with others;
- established and maintained trusting relationships and confidence in themselves and others;
- sought appreciation and recognition and in turn extended appreciation and recognition to others;
- sought a sense of caring, sharing and community and extended these things to others;
- established and maintained honest and open communications with all those in school;
- maintained high expectations for themselves and others;
- sought and extended collegiality;
- safeguarded what they regarded as important.

To this list we would add the following observations. First, that empowered teachers are able to convince themselves and others, through rational argument and action, that they are teaching something of value. Secondly, they recognise that the world of education, 'out there' can be overpowering. They appreciate that through hegemonic conditioning people *are* organised into power relationships but they do not accept that any alternative is impossible. They do not accept their professional predicament because it is in some way natural and unchangeable. They recognise the extent of those factors which constrain, marginalise and disempower them and actively question the order of things. Thirdly, empowered teachers are aware that critical reflection-on-practice might be perceived by other teachers in the school as cynicism and obstruction. Some teachers might describe it as 'rocking the boat' or 'sticking your head above the parapet'. Some teachers have to suffer taunts such as, 'You are not living in the real world!'. Fourthly, empowered teachers are 'critical' people capable of critical self-reflection and critical action (Barnett 1997). This critical disposition is an ability to size up the world in all its manifestations, to take it seriously, but not kowtow to it. Empowered teachers have the clarity of thinking and emotional strength to stand apart from what some regard as the 'real world' of teaching and show, in their actions, that there are other ways of understanding and teaching in this 'real world'. This is why some teachers neither relish having empowered or critically reflective practitioners on their staff. They find these colleagues unsettling. Their actions can generate resistance.

Critical reflection-on-practice needs to be seen as constructive action towards a better life. Teachers need to be open about what a better life looks like, and through debate and contestation be prepared to justify what they value and do. Critically reflective practitioners do not look at their professional lives in terms of what they are allowed to do, but what they can and want to do to improve teaching and learning in the school. An empowering school culture is always in motion. It modifies and reconstructs itself in the light of changing internal and external influences. It places children's learning centre stage and exhibits those cultural characteristics which continuously, not erratically, support teachers in the pursuit of shared and valued outcomes. Like the development of effective school partnerships, becoming critically reflective takes time, patience, openness and courage. Critically reflective practitioners are risk-takers, able to deal with the uncertainty and ambiguity that comes from exploring new ways of doing things. They flourish in schools where there is not a culture of blame when things appear to get worse before they get better, but in schools where there is a culture of pride. A pride that comes from knowing that there is a collective commitment to continuously strive to 'think again' and to improve the quality of children's educational experiences.

CHAPTER SEVEN

Reflections on the Whole: Thinking Again

Reflection-on-practice is an expression of a 'desire to think again' (Clandinin and Connelly 1995). Reflection is thinking again about teaching and learning. Some of the important attributes of this process are neatly summarised by Benita, a Canadian student teacher who wrote the following in her professional learning portfolio.

> I see myself as a reflective practitioner. I am a person who wonders and questions. I think about daily happenings in my classroom: what is going on with my students, how I am making sense of being a teacher, and how I am figuring out the curriculum.
> Portfolio entry, 5 June 1992 (quoted in Clandinin and Connelly 1995: 82)

'Thinking again' conveys the idea that reflection-on-practice needs to be seen as a continuous process of knowledge construction.

Thinking again: Adam's reflections-on-practice

Adam is a final year primary student undertaking an eight week school experience. As part of his course he has to conduct a piece of research into an aspect of teaching and learning. He has chosen to focus on the notion of 'being an effective teacher'. A central claim of his course is to enable him to become a reflective practitioner, skilled at interrogating his practice and learning from the evidence he gathers about his teaching. Adam keeps a reflective learning journal and has asked his pupils to do the same. He has worked hard in his first week's teaching to explain to his class how they might make entries in their journals. He has discussed issues of honesty, confidentiality and the reasons why he is asking them to do this. One of Adam's early entries is presented below. This provides a context for some of the things he claimed he learnt, which are given later. His reflections during his school experience show plenty of evidence of three types of reflection-on-practice we outlined in Chapter 2, namely descriptive, perceptive and receptive types. There is also some evidence of interactive reflection-on-practice. Adam writes:

The scene is a fairly typical classroom in an urban primary school located in an area of Victorian villas and houses built in the inter-war period. Children of Spanish, Irish, Italian, British, and other nationalities attend the school.

It is a bright, sunny Monday morning in the summer term. I enter room 2 just before the lesson, from assembly to breaktime, is due to start. I feel cheerful, expectant and looking forward to my class of Year 6 (10–11 year olds). Under one arm my visual aid, an old roll of patterned wallpaper with a large diagram on the reverse side showing the school in relation to a place in northern Queensland called Ravenswood. Under the other, a small portable projector, complete with an extension cable which I've wedged up under my armpit. In my right hand my briefcase with photographs to help convey the notion of a gold rush and handouts for all the children in the form of four pictures, in sequence, that reflect the changing fortunes of Ravenswood through time. In the other hand I have a carrier bag. Inside is a battery-powered cassette recorder – too many plugs and cables on the floor is not good news with this group. My tape is ready to turn and at the right place, I hope. Also in the bag is a copy of my lesson plan – carefully thought through, I think – a mug, jar of coffee, some dried milk and my potato.

I feel rather like a salesman with all this paraphernalia, a little like an ambassador (I'm a student on final teaching practice), and certainly like an anthropologist as I endeavour to undertake a piece of classroom-based, practitioner research (as part of my module called 'The Teacher as Researcher') that requires me to get inside this thing called school culture and explore how the children are making sense of their learning experiences with me. I want to know how effective they think my teaching is.

The bell goes, but there is no sign of the children. To fill the expanding silence I reach down into the carrier bag and begin to carve my initials on my potato. (Monday is potato day for staff. The potatoes go in the oven at breaktime and are devoured at lunch). No sooner done than the children enter the classroom, cheerful as usual. They always seem to be engaged in such earnest conversation. But here I am, 'student-anthropologist', slipping into my participant-observer role again. As usual they are never short of something to say as they pass my desk. 'You've had your hair cut, sir', 'Sorry we're late but Mr Springer (the Head) made us sing the hymn again because he said we weren't singing the words clearly enough', 'Did you have a nice weekend, sir?' 'Watch him today, sir, he's in a bad mood.' As they glide past I run through my much-practised looks which convey a sense of amusement, interest, slight embarrassment, and a measure of surprise.

As they settle in their places I begin my well-used opening move. It is a good exemplar of what Mehan (1979) would call a cooccurrence relationship. 'Good morning, everyone. Good to be with you again', 'Good morning, sir. Wish we could say the same.' So the lesson begins. It is about Man's use of scarce natural resources. First I read a short story, then turn off the lights to play some music from my record of the sound track from the film 'Paint your Wagon'. *In no time at all we are up on our magic carpet, travelling through time and across space to northern Queensland in the 1860s.*

After the lesson the student reminds the children of the procedures they have negotiated for writing up and sharing their thoughts and feelings about the lesson, through the medium of their individual reflective diaries. The student did this for the duration of his eight-week teaching practice. When he reflected on what his children wrote, he learnt many things about himself as a teacher. Some of the main things were:

1. Learning to see things from the pupils' point of view

I have learnt that my children are more than capable of reflecting on our work together. What they have written is very useful feedback on my teaching. Perhaps the most powerful thing I have learnt is that classroom action has a certain purpose and meaning. It has meaning for the teacher and for the child and the two are not always the same. What really matters is what the children are learning.

2. Being comfortable with different opinions about my lessons

My lesson evaluations are just one view of things. My class teacher's is another. The pupils have lots of different views as well. For example, in the Ravenswood lesson Paul found the whole thing easy but Michael found it hard. Michael has difficulties empathising and imagining while Abi found it easy and says why. Raj on the other hand thought the lesson was 'very good indeed' whereas Rachael thought it got 'more and more boring'. On reflection I have learnt that there is not just one 'reality' but many realities. What I need to do is learn to grasp reality as my children know it.

3. Appreciating that I often say one thing and do something else

I have learnt that if I value group work and children getting on, working things out for themselves, discussing, learning to compromise and see other people's point of view, then I have got to let go of things more, especially what I control and when. One of Joanne's journal entries really made me stop and think. She wrote, 'You tell us to get on with our work then every five minutes you stop us and tell us something. It's good in a way but we don't get much done if you keep talking.' This is something I need to work on. I want to hear the children talk but I haven't learnt when to shut up!

4. Acknowledging that children have clear views about what is a 'good' teacher

Comparing my reflections on my lessons with the pupils' view of things has been a really sobering experience! They have helped me to question why I have done certain things and my teaching itself. Some of the things that I didn't think were that important at the start of the teaching practice, I now see differently, and the children have helped me to appreciate this. I am now much more aware of the importance to children of explaining things clearly, of not breaking up the dynamics of group work when I think of something else to say, about writing in their books more legibly, of giving them reasons why I am asking them to do the activities I set them, the importance of using praise and of being consistent in my application of classroom rules.

Thinking again: Tony's reflections-on-practice

Tony is a teacher of Years 4–7 who is undertaking a taught Masters degree in the spirit of continuing his professional development. What follows is an extract from a reflective piece of writing where he is trying to make sense of his first years in the teaching profession. Evidence of all the different types of reflection-on-practice we outlined in Chapter 2 can be seen. In particular, Tony engages in critical reflection-on-practice as he questions the whole business of knowledge production and reproduction, questions the nature and role of 'theory' and juggles the diverse 'texts' of professional socialisation as he tries to develop a coherent philosophy which will enable him to act competently in the classroom.

I was trained as a teacher with geography as my subject specialism. I left college after four years of study with a Bachelor of Education degree, supposedly equipped to teach children from 8 to 13 years of age. My first job was in a school in Leicestershire. It was a period of survival but it was also a time of discovery. One of my major preoccupations of that time was a question, 'How can I support and facilitate my pupils' learning when I am somewhat bewildered and uncertain about what is actually happening in my classroom?' Some of my reflections on my practice went like this. They are a reconstruction based on my own lived experiences.

I left college thinking that I should have a healthy respect for those robust and complicated things called theories. Lengthy lectures about Ausbelian advanced organisers, Piagetian stages, Brunerian spirals, Gagné's types of learning, Rumelhart and

Norman's information processing, about Freud and Jung, and so on, led me to believe that educational theory was related to educational practice, my practice. Additionally, because I believed that those bodies of knowledge were put together systematically and over time by respected academics, then they would have the power to explain what was happening in my classroom, I put a lot of faith and trust in them.

But very soon things started to happen which initially led me to think that something was seriously wrong with me, the children, the activities or, even worse, the whole learning milieu in my classroom. For example, I was finding that some children were very good at solving practical science-type problems when working on the topics of rocks and soils, but less good at understanding that places were located in both space and time. I found that some children were very good at creative writing when we were exploring the experiences of those living in hazardous environments and yet they were still counting on their fingers when we were doing exercises requiring graphicacy and numeracy. I found that some children wanted the freedom to learn and to express themselves in their own way when we were exploring the neighbourhood, but wanted lots of structure and guidance in order to be able to write an engaging story.

And what about my own teaching? In short, when I appealed to theory and tried to relate it to what was actually going on in my classroom full of unpredictability, multidimensionality and simultaneity, I discovered two things. First, the theory did not fit my particular situation: even if I tried to force-fit it, it did not fit. Secondly, it did not help to explain my practice, to enable me to offer explanations for what was going on. As a newly qualified teacher I needed to feel confident that the profession, which had just acquired a new member, possessed educational theory which could relate directly to educational practice in classrooms. For the first five years of my career I had a crisis of confidence. All this so-called 'knowledge' seemed to have no direct relevance to my practical everyday pedagogical problems.

Later in his account Tony reflects on his practice and in so doing begins to make good sense of it. Reflection helps Tony to 'add value' to his existing understandings. He writes:

I want to extend and elaborate upon some of the things I claim I learnt from these early and very formative 'beginning' years as a teacher. I held a number of debilitating beliefs. First, I had too much respect for the knowledge generated by others. I did not question it. By implication I devalued my own knowledge. I can remember asking myself the question, 'So why doesn't my knowledge count as much as yours?' I was beginning to learn that knowledge was 'positioned' (Hollingsworth 1994). There seemed to be a kind of high-status knowledge and then there was my knowledge. I felt that my knowledge did not count as much as that knowledge I was reading about in books and written largely by people working in institutions of higher education. Secondly, I did not believe that knowledge could be seen as a 'contested terrain'. Perhaps, rather naively, I thought knowledge from 'outside' was relevant and appropriate. If it did not appear to be so then the problem rested with me, not with the nature of this knowledge.

Thirdly, I believed that I could facilitate children's learning even though I could not claim to understand and enhance my own learning: this was misguided and presumptuous. Fourthly, I believed that because I felt able to explain things clearly to children, I could naturally talk clearly about my practice to other teachers. I was in fact very inarticulate and unable to explain my most sacred and cherished work patterns and values when called upon to do so. I was unable to transform contextualised experience into decontextualised discourse.

Finally, I believe that if I looked at my pupils I would understand what they were learning. On reflection I needed to shift from looking and make more effort to listen to my pupils. The conflict I experienced between my beliefs and my practice gave me the motivation to continue my professional development by looking specifically at my values and my values-in-action, on the one hand, and the idea of coming to know my own practice, on the other.

In this book we have tried to convey reflection-on-practice as a process of continuous knowledge construction. This has meant two things. First, that teachers need to be regarded as active, creative individuals, with an ability to think through the possibilities and probable consequences of a line of action, for example, a lesson, in the light of their experience of teaching other lessons. Relative practitioners are 'educators with a purpose, able to take control over their own futures ...' (Calderhead and Shorrock 1997: 16). Secondly, it means that teachers have an ability to construct a professional world that is meaningful to them. These understandings and insights are often 'local' and grounded in one classroom or school. They may also be fragmentary in the sense that we can never claim to 'know it all'. We can never claim to know ourselves and our teaching in a complete, consistent and uncomplicated way (Ghaye 1986). Reflection linked to this constructionist view is essentially a liberating message. It means that reality is not fixed or given but that teachers partake in its creation. Reflection-on-practice helps us to keep our options open, to seek fresh alternatives and consolidate our learning. But there is another message also: to do with commitment. It is a commitment, willingness and enthusiasm to question the knowledge that is created, to challenge personal and collective values and to interrogate the contradictions and paradoxes that appear from the construction of teachers' professional knowledge.

We have also argued that at the heart of the reflective process is the reflective conversation. We have taken Schön's original idea (1983) and extended it. Originally Schön referred to this as part of reflection-in-action where professionals try to solve their reframed problems. He described this process as a 'conversation with the situation'. In extending this idea our thinking has been greatly influenced by Freire (1972) and Whitehead (1993) amongst others. Meaningful reflective conversations can sustain and nourish us. They can raise individual and collective consciousness. Above all else they involve a discussion of values. This is at the heart of the improvement process. In this sense, reflective conversations are those of:

- *possibility*: if they contain reference not only to what was felt, thought and done but what might come to be in terms of valued outcomes;
- *confrontation*: if they serve to interrogate and question teaching and learning and avoid celebrating it uncritically;
- *hope*: if the valued outcomes are to do with trying to bring about relevant, principled and ethically-grounded improvements in teaching and learning in schools.

Reflection-on-practice is the way teachers attempt to improve the existing order and pattern of things. It is a vital part of a teacher's meaning-making process. When so many are buffeted by the forces of change, reflection-on-practice can help teachers regain some sense of control over their lives. When accounts of teaching contain repeated reference to professional turbulence and chaos, reflection can help them discern some order and pattern within the chaos, for teaching and learning is a universe of patterns.

> Every night the stars move in circles across the sky. The seasons cycle at yearly intervals. No two snowflakes are ever exactly the same, but they all have a sixfold symmetry. Tigers and zebras are covered in patterns of stripes, leopards and hyenas are covered in patterns of spots. Intricate trains of waves march across the oceans; very similar trains of sand dunes march across the desert. Coloured arcs of light adorn the sky in the form of rainbows, and a bright circular halo sometimes surrounds the moon on winter nights ... Patterns possess utility as well as beauty. Once we have learned to recognise a background pattern, exceptions suddenly stand out. The desert stands still but the lion moves.
>
> (Stewart 1995: 1–3)

References

Ackoff, R. (1979) 'The future of operational research is past', *Journal of Operational Research Society* **30**(2), 93–104.

Argyris, C. and Schön D. (1992) *Theory in Practice: Increasing Professional Effectiveness*. San Francisco: Jossey Bass.

Ashcroft, K. and Griffiths, M. (1989) 'Reflective teachers and reflective tutors: school experience in an Initial Teacher Education Course', *Journal of Education for Teaching* **15**(1), 35–52.

Ashton, E. (1997) 'Investigating the Nature of Values: Agreed or Transcendent?' Paper presented at the Conference on Values and the Curriculum, Institute of Education, University of London, 10–11 April, 1997.

Barnett, R. (1997) *Higher Education: A Critical Business*. Buckingham: Open University Press.

Baumeister, R. (1991) *Meanings of Life*. New York: Guilford Press.

Bengtsson, J. (1995) 'What is reflection? On reflection in the teaching profession and teacher education', *Teachers and Teaching: Theory and Practice* **1**(1), 23–32.

Benner, P. (1984) *From Novice to Expert*. New York: Addison-Wesley.

Borko, H. and Mayfield, V. (1995) 'The roles of the cooperating teacher and university supervisor in learning to teach', *Teaching and Teacher Education* **11**, 501–518.

Boud, D. and Miller, N. (1996) *Working with Experience: Animating Learning*. London: Routledge.

Boud, D., Keogh, R., Walker, D. (1985) 'Promoting reflection in learning: a model', in Boud, D., Keogh, R., Walker, D. (eds), (1985) *Reflection: Turning Experience into Learning*. New York: Kogan Page.

Bourd, D., Cohen, R., Walker, D. (eds), (1997) *Using Experience for Learning*. Buckingham: SRHE and Open University Press.

Bourdieu, P. (1994) *Reproduction in Education, Society and Culture*. London: Sage Publications.

Brookfield, S. (1995) *Developing Critical Thinkers: Challenging Adults to Explore Alternative Ways of Thinking and Acting*. Buckingham: Open University Press.

Brown, A. (1995) *Organisational Culture*. London: Pitman Publishing Company.

Burr, V. (1995) *An Introduction to Social Constructionism*. London: Routledge.

Calderhead, J. and Gates, P. (eds) (1993), *Conceptualising Reflection in Teacher Development*. London: Falmer Press.

Campbell, A. and Kane, I. (1996) 'Mentoring and primary school culture', in McIntyre, D. and Hagger, H. (eds) (1996), *Mentors in Schools: Developing the Profession of Teaching*. London: David Fulton Publishers.

Carey, G. (1997) 'Moral values – the challenge and the opportunity'. Unpublished Paper presented at the Values and the Curriculum Conference, Institute of Education, University of London, 10–11 April 1997.

Carr, W. (1987) 'What is an educational practice?' *Journal of Philosophy of Education* **21**(2), 167–80.

Carr, W. (1989) 'Introduction: Understanding Quality in Teaching', in *Quality in Teaching: Arguments for a Reflective Profession*. London: Falmer Press.

Carr, D. (1992) 'Practical enquiry, values and the problem of educational theory', *Oxford Review of Education* **18**(3), 241–51.

Carr, W. (1995) *For Education: Towards Critical Educational Inquiry*. Buckingham: Open University Press.

Carr, W. and Kemmis, S. (1986) *Becoming Critical: Education, Knowledge and Action Research*. London: The Falmer Press.

Chittenden, A. (1993) 'How can a pastoral care programme improve a school culture?' *Pastoral Care in Education* **11**, 3.

Clandinin, J. (1995) 'Still learning to teach', in Russell, T. and Korthagen, F. (eds) (1995) *Teachers who Teach Teachers: Reflections on Teacher Education*. London: The Falmer Press.

Clandinin, J. and Connelly, M. (1995) *Teachers' Professional Knowledge Landscapes*. New York: Teachers' College Press.

Cunnah, W., Phillips, R., Richards, S. (1997) 'Counting the costs or realising the profits? Partnerships, politics and professional development, *British Journal of In-Service Education* **23**(2), 145–61.

Curran, C. (1997) 'Whose needs first? An exploration of the value systems underpinning arrangements for Primary-Secondary transfer'. Paper presented at the Conference on Values and the Curriculum, Institute of Education, University of London, 10–11 April 1997.

Day, C. (1987) 'Professional learning through collaborative in-service activity', in Smyth, J. (ed.) (1987) *Educating Teachers: Changing the Nature of Pedagogical Knowledge*. London: Falmer Press.

Day, C. (1991) 'Professional Development and Change in the 1990s: Issues for Action Researchers'. Opening address presented at the Collaborative Action Research Network International Conference, University of Nottingham, UK, 19–21 April 1991.

Denzin, N. (1997) *Interpretative Ethnography: Ethnographic Practices for the 21st Century*. Thousand Oaks, CA: Sage Publications.

Department for Education (DfE) (1992a) *Administrative Memorandum 8/92, Initial Teacher Training (Secondary Phase)*. London: DfE.

Department for Education (DfE) (1992b) *Initial Teacher Training (Secondary Phase)*. Circular 9/92. London: DfE.

Department for Education (DfE) (1993a) *The Initial Training of Primary School Teachers: New Criteria for Courses*. Circular 14/93. London: DfE.

Department for Education (DfE) (1993b) *The Initial Teacher Training of Primary School Teachers: New Criteria for Course Approval*, Circular 16/93. London: DfE.

Department for Education and Employment (DfEE) (1997) *Standards for the Award of Qualified Teacher Status* (prepared by the Teacher Training Agency), June, (1997).

Department for Education and Employment (DfEE) (1998a) *Induction for New Teachers: A Consultation Document*. London: DfEE.

Department for Education and Employment (DfEE) (1998b) *Teaching: High Status, High Standards, Requirements for Courses of Initial Teacher Training*. London: DfEE.

Dewey, J. (1933) *How we Think: A Restatement of the Relation of Reflective Thinking to the Educative Process*. Chicago: Henry Regnery Publishers.

Diamond, P. (1991) *Teacher Education as Transformation*. Milton Keynes: Open University Press.

Dunne E. and Bennett, N. (1997) 'Mentoring processes in school-based training', *British Educational Research Journal* **23**(2), 225–37.

Edwards, A. (1996) 'Can action research give coherence to the school-based learning of experiences of students?' in O'Hanlon, C. (ed.) (1996) *Professional Development Through Action Research in Educational Settings*. London: Falmer Press.

Elliott, J. (1987) 'Educational theory, practical philosophy and action research', *British Journal of Educational Studies* **35**, 149–69.

Elliott, J. (1994) 'Clarifying values in schools', *The Cambridge Journal of Education* **24**(3), 413–22.

Elliott, J. (1997) 'School-based curriculum development and action research in the United Kingdom', in Hollingsworth, S. (ed.) (1997) *International Action Research: A Casebook for Educational Reform*. London: Falmer Press.

Elliott, J., MacLure, M., Sarland, C. (1996) *Teachers as Researchers in the Context of Award Bearing Courses and Research Degrees*. CARE and the School of Education and Professional Development, University of East Anglia, UK.

Eraut, M. (1994a) 'Indicators and accountability at the school and classroom level', in *Making Education Count: Developing and Using International Indicators*. Paris: Organisation for Economic Cooperation and Development, 289–306.

Eraut, M. (1994b) *Developing Professional Knowledge and Competence*. London: Falmer Press.

Eraut, M. (1995a) 'Developing professional knowledge within a client-centred orientation', in Guskey, T. and Huberman, M. (eds) (1995) *Professional Development in Education: New Paradigms and Practices*. New York: Teachers' College Press.

Eraut, M. (1995b) 'Schön shock: a case for reframing reflection-in-action', *Teachers and Teaching: Theory and Practice* **1**(1), 9–22.

Fairclough, N. (1998) *Discourse and Social Change*, Cambridge: Polity Press.

Fosnot, C. (ed.) (1996) *Constructivism: Theory, Perspectives and Practice*, New York: Teachers' College Press.

Fowler, K. (1997) 'Partners in the Partnership: Evaluation of supervision of final school experience for students placed in schools in Hereford and Worcester who are in partnership with Worcester College of Higher Education'. Unpublished thesis for the degree of BA(Ed) (Hons), University of Coventry.

Freire, P. (1972) *Pedagogy of the Oppressed*. Harmondsworth: Penguin.

Fullan, M. (1994) *Change Forces: Probing the Depths of Educational Reform*. London: The Falmer Press.

Furlong, J. *et al.* (1996) 'Re-defining partnership: revolution or reform in initial teacher education?' *Journal of Education for Teaching* **22**(1), 39–55.

Galton, M., Simon, B., Croll, P. (1980) *Inside the Primary Classroom*. London: Routledge and Kegan Paul.

Garman, N. (1995) 'The schizophrenic rhetoric of school reform and the effects on teacher development', in Smyth, J. (ed.) (1995), *Critical Discourses on Teacher Development*. London: Cassell.

Ghaye, T. (1986) 'Pupil typifications of topic work', *British Educational Research Journal* **12**(2), 125–35.

Ghaye, T., Johnstone, E., Jones, J. (1993) *Assessment and the Management of Learning*. Leamington Spa: Scholastic Publications.

Ghaye, T. and Wakefield, P. (eds) (1993) *CARN Critical Conversations: A Trilogy, Book One: The Role of Self in Action Research*. Dorset: Hyde Publications.

Ghaye, T. (ed.) (1995) *CARN Critical Conversations: A Trilogy, Book Three: Creating Cultures for Improvement: Dialogues, Decisions and Dilemmas*. Dorset: Hyde Publications.

Ghaye, T. *et al.* (1996a) *An Introduction to Learning through Critical Reflective Practice*. Newcastle-upon-Tyne: Pentaxion Press.

Ghaye, T. *et al.* (1996b) *Theory-Practice Relationships: Reconstructing Practice*. Newcastle-upon-Tyne: Pentaxion Press.

Ghaye, T. and Lillyman, S. (1997) *Learning Journals and Critical Incidents: Reflective Practice for Health Care Professionals, Key Management Skills in Nursing*. Salisbury: Mark Allen Publishing.

Giroux, H. (1987) 'Educational reform and the politics of teacher empowerment', *New Era* **9**(1–2), 3–13.

Gitlin, A. and Russell, R. (1994) 'Alternative methodologies and the research context', in Gitlin, A. (ed.) (1994) *Power and Method: Political Activism and Educational Research*. London: Routledge.

Gleick, J. (1988) *Making a New Science*. New York: Heinemann.

Glover, D. and Mardle, G. (1996) 'Issues in the management of mentoring', in McIntyre, D. and Hagger, H. (eds) (1996), *Mentors in Schools: Developing the Profession of Teaching*. London: David Fulton Publishers.

Goldhammer, R. (1966) 'A critical analysis of spuervision of instruction in the Harvard-Lexington Summer programme'. Unpublished PhD thesis, Harvard University.

Goodson, I. (1997) '"Trendy Theory" and Teacher Professionalism', in Hargreaves A. and Evans, R. (eds) (1997) *Beyond Educational Reform: Bringing Teachers Back In*. Buckingham: Open University Press.

Gore, J. and Zeichner, K. (1995) 'Connecting action research to genuine teacher development', in Smyth, J. (ed.) (1995) *Critical Discourses on Teacher Development*. London: Cassell.

Gramsci, A. (1971) *Selections from Prison Notebooks*. New York: New Left Books.

Great Britain. Parliament. House of Commons (1997) *Excellence in Schools* (cm 3681). London: HMSO.

Great Britain. Statutes. (1988) *Education Reform Act 1988*, Chapter 40. London: HMSO.

Greene, M. (1986) 'Reflection and passion in teaching', *Journal of Curriculum and Supervision* **2**(1), 68–81.

Hagger, H., Burn, K., McIntyre, D. 91995) *The School Mentor Handbook*. London: Kogan Page.

Halstead, J. and Taylor, M. (eds) (1996) *Values in Education and Education in Values*. London: Falmer Press.

Harre, R. and Gillett, G. (1994) *The Discursive Mind*. Thousand Oaks, CA: Sage Publications.

Haydon, G. (1997) *Teaching About Values: A New Approach*. London: Cassell.

Henry, C. (1991) 'If action research were tennis', in Zuber-Skerritt, O. (ed.) (1991) *Action Learning for Improved Performance*. Brisbane: AEBIS Publishing.

Henry, C. (1993) 'McDonald's, Republicanism and Botham's early departure: democratic education for a change?' in Ghaye, T. and Wakefield, P. (eds) (1993) *CARN Critical Conversations: A Trilogy, The Role of Self in Action Research*. Dorset: Hyde Publications.

Hill, D. (1997) 'Equality in primary schooling: the policy context, intentions and effects of the Conservative "reforms"', in Cole, M., Hill, D., Shan, S. (eds) *Promoting Equality in Primary Schools*. London: Cassell.

Hollingsworth, S. (1994) 'Repositioning the teacher in US schools and society: feminist readings of action research'. Unpublished Paper presented at the CARN International Conference, University of Birmingham, UK.

Hollingsworth, S. (ed.) (1997) *International Action Research: A Casebook for Educational Reform*. London: Falmer Press.

Holly, M-L. (1989) *Writing to Grow: Keeping a Personal Professional Journal*. Portsmouth, NH: Heinemann.

Hursh, D. (1992) 'Re-politicising pedagogy: developing ethically and critically reflective teachers within the liberal discourse of teacher education programmes', *Critical Pedagogy Networker* **5**, 1–7.

Husbands, C. 91993) 'Profiling of student teachers: Context, ownership and the beginnings of professional learning', in Bridges, D. and Kerry, T. (eds) (1993) *Developing Teachers Professionally*. London: Routledge.

Hutchinson, D. (1994) 'Competence-based profiles for ITT and Induction: the place of reflection', *British Journal of In-Service Education* **20**(3), 303–312.

Jackson, P., Boostrom, R., Hansen, D. (1993) *The Moral Life of Schools*. San Francisco: Jossey Bass.

Johnson, R. and Redmond, D. (1998) *The Art of Empowerment: The profit and pain of employee involvement*. London: Pitman Publishing.

Johnston, S. (1988) 'Towards an understanding of the values issue in curriculum decision-making', *School Organisation* **8**(1), 51–7.

Kemmis, S. and McTaggart, R. (1988a) *The Action Research Planner*. Geelong, South Australia: Deakin University Press.

Kemmis, S. and McTaggart, R. (eds) (1988b) *The Action Research Reader*. Geelong, South Australia: Deakin University Press.

Kolb, D. (1984) *Experiential Learning: Experience as the Source of Learning and Development*. New Jersey: Prentice Hall.

Lee, S. and Wilkes, J. (1996) 'The changing role of the school experience tutor', *British Journal of In-Service Education* **22**(1), 99–112.

Lehane, T. (1992) 'Wet Tuesday afternoons at Shireton School: How can I enhance the everyday school experiences of children with profound and multiple learning difficulties and those who work with them?'. Unpublished MEd thesis, Worcester College of Higher Education, UK.

Lewin, K. (1946) 'Action research and minority problems', *Journal of Social Issues* **2**, 34–46.

Lewis, T. (1993) 'Valid knowledge and the problem of practical arts curricula', *Curriculum Inquiry* **23**(2), 175–202.

Lomax, P. (ed.) (1996) *Quality Management in Education: Sustaining the Vision through Action Research*. London: Routledge and Hyde Publications.

Lomax, P. and Selley, N. (1996) 'Supporting critical communities through an educational action research network'. Presentation from the Kingston Hill Action Research Group for the BEMAS Research Conference, Cambridge, (1996) Kingston Upon Thames, Kingston Hill Publications.

Lomax, P., Whitehead, J., Evans, M. (1996) 'Contributing to an epistemology of quality management practice', in Lomax, P. (ed.) (1996) *Quality Management in Education: Sustaining the Vision through Action Research*. London: Routledge and Hyde Publications.

Mardle, G. (1995) 'The consequences' (Chapter 9), in Glover, D. and Mardle, G. (eds) (1995), *The Management of Mentoring: Policy Issues*. London: Kogan Page.

McGill, I. and Beaty, L. (1996) *Action Learning*. London: Kogan Page.

McIntyre D. and Hagger, H. (1996) 'Mentoring: challenges for the future', in McIntyre, D. and Hagger, H. (eds) (1996), *Mentors in Schools: Developing the Profession of Teaching*. London: David Fulton Publishers.

McKernan, J. (1996) *Curriculum Action Research: A Handbook of Methods and Resources for the Reflective Practitioner*. London: Kogan Page.

McLaren, P. (1989) *Schooling as a Ritual Performance*. London: Routledge and Kegan Paul.

McNiff, J. (1991) *Action Research: Principles and Practice*. Basingstoke: Macmillan Education Limited.

McNiff, J., Lomax, P., Whitehead, J. (1996) *You and Your Action Research Project*. London: Routledge and Hyde Publications.

McNiff, J., Whitehead, J., Laidlaw, M. (1992) *Creating a Good Social Order Through Action Research*. Dorset: Hyde Publications.

McPeck, J. (1990) *Teaching Critical Thinking*. New York: Routledge.

Mehan, H. (1979) *Learning Lessons: Social Organisation in the Classroom*. Cambridge, Mass.: Harvard University Press.

Melenyzer, A. (1991) 'Teacher empowerment: narrative of the silenced practitioners'. Unpublished PhD thesis, Indiana University of Pennsylvania, USA.

Miller, J. (1990) *Creating Spaces and Finding Voices*. New York: SUNY.

Miller, N. and Boud, D. (1996) 'Animating learning from experience', in Boud, D. and Miller, N. (eds) (1996) *Working with Experience: Animating Learning*. London: Routledge.

Morrison, D. (1997) 'Cultural Values: Human Rights, Religion and the Curriculum', Paper presented at the Conference on Values and the Curriculum, Institute of Education, University of London, 10–11 April, 1997.

Munby H. and Russell, T. (1995) 'Towards rigour with relevance: How teachers and teacher educators claim to know?', in Russell, T. and Korthagen, F. (eds) (1995) *Teachers Who Teach Teachers: Reflections on Teacher Education*. London: Falmer Press.

National Curriculum Council (NCC) (1991) *Curriculum Matters 5: Health Education*. London: NCC.

Newman, F. and Holzman, L. (1997) *The End of Knowing: A New Developmental Way of Knowing*. London: Routledge.

Nicholls, G. (1997) *Collaborative Change in Education*. London: Kogan Page.

Nixon, J. (1995) 'Teaching as a profession of values', in Smyth, J. (ed.) (1995) *Critical Discourses on Teacher Development*. London: Cassell.

Noffke, S. (1997) 'Themes and tensions in US action research: towards historical analysis', in Hollingsworth, S. (ed.) (1997) *International Action Research: A Casebook for Educational Reform*. London: Falmer Press.

O'Hanlon, C. (ed.) (1996) *Professional Development through Action Research in Educational Settings*. London: Falmer Press.

Office for Standards in Education (OFSTED) (1995a) *Framework for the Inspection of Nursery, Primary, Middle, Secondary and Special Schools*. London: HMSO.

Office for Standards in Education (OFSTED) (1995b) *Partnership: Schools and Higher Education in Partnership in Secondary Initial Teacher Training*. London: HMSO.

Olsen, J. (1992) *Understanding Teaching*. Milton Keynes: Open University Press.

Parker, S. (1997) *Reflective Teaching in the Postmodern World: A Manifesto for Education in Postmodernity*. Buckingham: Open University Press.

Paul, R. (1990) *Critical Thinking: What Every Person Needs to Survive in a Rapidly Changing World*. California: Rohnert Park.

Pendlebury, S. (1995) 'Reason and story in wise practice', in McEwan, H. and Egan, K. (eds) (1995) *Narrative in Teaching, Learning and Research*. New York: Teachers' College Press.

Pheysey, D. (1993) *Organisational Cultures: Types and Transformations*. London: Routledge.

Polanyi, M. (1958) *Personal Knowledge*. Oxford: Oxford University Press.

Polanyi, M. (1962) *Personal Knowledge: Towards a Post-critical Philosophy*. New York: Harper and Row.

Pollard, A. (ed.) (1996) *Readings for Reflective Teaching in the Primary School*. London: Cassell.

Pollard, A. (1997) *Reflective Teaching in the Primary School: A Handbook for the Classroom*. London: Cassell.

Pollard, A. and Triggs, P. (1997) *Reflective Teaching in Secondary Education*. London: Cassell.

Prilleltensky, I. and Fox, D. (1997) 'Introducing critical psychology: values, assumptions and the status quo', in Fox, D. and Prilleltensky, I. (eds) (1997) *Critical Psychology: An Introduction*. London: Sage Publications.

Pring, R. (1988) 'Confidentiality and the right to know', in Murphy, R. and Torrance, H. (eds) (1988), *Evaluating Education: Issues and Methods*. London: Paul Chapman.

Ratuva, S. (1997) 'In search of common values: Construction of ethnicist values, disempowerment and civil society responses in Fiji'. Paper presented at the Conference on Values and the Curriculum, Institute of Education, University of London, 10–11 April, 1997.

Ravn, I. (1991) 'What should guide reality construction?' in Steier, F. (ed.) (1991) *Research and Reflexivity*. London: Sage Publications.

Richardson, V. (ed.) (1997) *Constructivist Teacher Education: Building a World of New Understandings*. London: Falmer Press.

Runnymede Bulletin (1997) 'A new vision for Britian', *Runnymede Bulletin*, 306.

Sarland, C. (1995) 'Action Research: Some British Funded Projects: A Review', Paper presented at the International Conference on Teacher Research, Davis, California, 13–15 April, 1995.

Scarth, J. and Hammersley, M. (1993) 'Questioning ORACLE: an assessment of ORACLE's analysis of teachers' questions', in Gomm, R. and Woods, P. (eds) (1993) *Educational Research in Action*. London: Paul Chapman Publishing in association with the Open University.

Schein, E. (1969) 'The mechanisms of change', in Bennis, W. (ed.) (1969) *Planning Change*. New York: Holt, Reinhart and Winston.

Schön, D. (1983) *The Reflective Practitioner: How Professionals Think in Action*. New York: Basic Books.

Schön, D. (1987) *Educating the Reflective Practitioner*. London: Jossey Bass.

Schön, D. (ed.) (1991) *The Reflective Turn: Case Studies in and on Educational Practice*. New York: Teachers' College Press.

School Curriculum and Assessment Authority (SCAA) (1996) *The National Forum for Values in Education and the Community: Final Report and Recommendations*. SCAA 96/43. London: SCAA.

Scott, C., Jaffe, D., Tobe, G. (1993) *Organisational Vision, Values and Mission*. New York: Crisp Publications.

Silcock, P. (1994) 'The process of reflective teaching', *British Journal of Educational Studies* **42**(3), 273–85.

Simpson, G. (1990) 'Keep it alive: elements of school culture that sustain innovation', *Educational Leadership* **47**(8), 34–7.

Smyth, J. (1991) *Teachers as Collaborative Learners*. Milton Keynes: Open University Press.

Smyth, J. (ed.) (1995) *Critical Discourses in Teacher Development*. London: Cassell.

Snyder, K. (1988) 'Managing a productive school work culture', *NASSP Bulletin* **72**(510), 40–43.

Stake, R. (1995) *The Art of Case Study Research*. London: Sage Publications.

Steinmaker, N. and Bell, N. (1979) *The Experiential Taxonomy: A New Approach to Teaching and Learning*. London: Academic Press.

Stenhouse, L. (1968) 'The Humanities Curriculum Project', *Journal of Curriculum Studies* **1**, 26–33.

Stenhouse, L. (1975) *An Introduction to Curriculum Research and Development*. London: Heinemann.

Stenhouse, L. (1981) 'What counts as research?' *British Journal of Educational Studies* **XXXIX**(2), June.

Stenhouse, L. (1983) *Authority, Education and Emancipation*. London: Heinemann Educational Books.

Stenhouse, L. (ed.) (1980) *Curriculum Development in Action*. London: Heinemann Educational Books.

Stevens, R. (1996) 'Introduction: Making sense of the person in a social world', in Stevens, R. (ed.) (1996) *Understanding the Self*. Milton Keynes: Open University.

Stewart, I. (1995) *Nature's Numbers: Discovering Order and Pattern in the Universe*. London: Weidenfeld and Nicolson.

Sumara, D. and Luce-Kapler, R. (1993) 'Action research as a writerly text; locating co-labouring in collaboration', *Educational Action Research* **1**, 387–95.

Taylor, I. (1997) Developing Learning in Professional Education: Partnerships for Practice. Buckingham: SRHE and Open University Press.

Teacher Training Agency (TTA) (1996/97) *Open Minds, Open Doors*. London: TTA,

Teacher Training Agency (TTA) (1997a) *Invitation to Bid for TTA INSET Funds, Annex B,* November 1997.

Teacher Training Agency (TTA) (1997b) *Career Entry Profile for Newly Qualified Teachers*. London: TTA.

Thomas, D. (1992) 'Putting Nature to the Rack : Narrative Studies as Research'. Paper presented at the Teacher's Stories of Life and Work Conference, Chester, UK.

Thomas, D. (ed.) (1995) *Teachers' Stories*. Buckingham: Open University Press.

Thompson, M. (1997) *Professional Ethics and the Teacher: Towards a General Teaching Council*. Stoke-on-Trent: Trentham Books.

Totterdell, M. (1997) 'The moralization of teaching: a relational approach as an ethical framework in the professional preparation and formation of teachers'. Paper presented at the Conference on Values and the Curriculum, Institute of Education, University of London, 10–11 April, 1997.

Tsang, N. (1998) 'Re-examining reflection – a common issue of professional concern in social work, teacher and nurse education', *Journal of Interprofessional Care* **12**(1), 21–31.

Tye, K. (1974) 'The culture of the school', in Goodlad, J. *et al.* (eds) *Toward a Mankind School: An Adventure in Humanistic Education*. New York: McGraw-Hill.

Valli, L. (1993) 'Reflective teacher education programs: an analysis of case studies', in Calderhead, J. and Gates, P. (eds) (1993) *Conceptualising Reflection in Teacher Development*. London: Falmer Press.

Wagner, A. (1987) '"Knots" in teachers' thinking', in Calderhead, J. (ed.) (1987) *Exploring Teachers' Thinking*. London: Cassell Education.

Weick, K. (1995) *Sensemaking in Organisations*. London: Sage Publications

Weil, S. and McGill, I. (eds) (1990) *Making Sense of Experiential Learning: Diversity in Theory and Practice*. Milton Keynes: SRHE and the Open University.

Weiler, K. (1988) *Women Teaching for Change, Gender, Class and Power*. South Hadley, MA: Bergin and Garvey Publishers.

Whitehead, J. (1985) 'The analysis of an individual's educational development', in Shipman, M. (ed.) *Educational Research: Principles, Policies and Practice*. London: Falmer Press.

Whitehead, J. (1989) 'Creating a living educational theory from questions of the kind, "How do I improve my practice?"', *Cambridge Journal of Education* **19**(1), 41–52.

Whitehead, J. (1992) *An Account of an Individual's Educational Development*. Action Research Group, School of Education: University of Bath, UK.

Whitehead, J. (1993) *The Growth of Educational Knowledge: Creating your own Living Educational Theories*. Bournemouth: Hyde Publications.

Whitehead, J. (1996) 'Living my values more fully in my practice', in Lomax, P. and Selley, N. (eds) (1996) *Supporting Critical Communities Through an Educational Action Research Network*. Kingston Hill Action Research Group, Kingston University, UK.

Whitehead, J. (1997) 'An original contribution to educational knowledge and professionalism'. A commentary on two Papers presented at AERA, Chicago, 1997, in Lomax, P. (1997) Kingston Hill Research Papers, No. 1. 37–49.

Whitty, G., Barton, L., Pollard, A. (1987) 'Ideology and control in teacher education: a review of recent experience in England', in Popkewitz, T. (ed.) (1987) *Critical Studies in Teacher Education: Its Folklore, Theory and Practice*. London: Falmer Press.

Woods, D. (1994) *Problem-based Learning: How to gain the most from PBL*. Hamilton, Ontario: McMaster University Press.

Wu, J. (1998) 'School Culture and its Impact on the Competence of Newly Qualified Teachers in Britain: Implications for China'. Unpublished doctoral thesis, University College Worcester, UK.

Wyness, M. and Silcock, P. (1997) 'Market Values, Primary Schooling and the Pupils' Perspective'. Paper presented at the Conference on Values and the Curriculum, Institute of Education, University of London, 10–11 April, 1997.

Young, R. (1992) *Critical Theory and Classroom Talk*. Clevedon: Multilingual Matters.

Zeichner, K. and Liston, D. (1996) *Reflective Teaching: An Introduction*. New Jersey: Lawrence Erlbaum Associates.

Zuber-Skerritt, O. (ed.) (1996) *New Directions in Action Research*. London: Falmer Press.

Index